VISUAL MODELING WITH RATIONAL ROSE AND UML

The Addison-Wesley Object Technology Series

Grady Booch, Ivar Jacobson, and James Rumbaugh, Series Editors

For more information check out the series web site [http://www.awl.com /cseng/otseries/] as well as the pages on each book [http://www.awl.com/cseng/I-S-B-N/] (I-S-B-N represents the actual ISBN, including dashes).

David Bellin and Susan Suchman Simone,
The CRC Card Book
ISBN 0-201-89535-8

Grady Booch, *Object Solutions: Managing the Object-Oriented Project*
ISBN 0-8053-0594-7

Grady Booch, *Object-Oriented Analysis and Design with Applications, Second Edition*
ISBN 0-8053-5340-2

Don Box, *Essential COM*
ISBN 0-201-63446-5

Alistair Cockburn, *Surviving Object-Oriented Projects: A Manager's Guide*
ISBN 0-201-49834-0

Dave Collins, *Designing Object-Oriented User Interfaces*
ISBN 0-8053-5350-X

Bruce Powel Douglass, *Real-Time UML: Developing Efficient Objects for Embedded Systems*
ISBN 0-201-32579-9

Desmond F. D'Souza and Alan Cameron Wills,
Objects, Components, and Frameworks with UML: The Catalysis Approach
ISBN 0-201-31012-0

Martin Fowler, *Analysis Patterns: Reusable Object Models*
ISBN 0-201-89542-0

Martin Fowler with Kendall Scott, *UML Distilled: Applying the Standard Object Modeling Language*
ISBN 0-201-32563-2

Peter Heinckiens, *Building Scalable Database Applications: Object-Oriented Design, Architectures, and Implementations*
ISBN 0-201-31013-9

Ivar Jacobson, Maria Ericsson, and Agenta Jacobson,
The Object Advantage: Business Process Reengineering with Object Technology
ISBN 0-201-42289-1

Ivar Jacobson, Magnus Christerson, Patrik Jonsson, and Gunnar Overgaard, *Object-Oriented Software Engineering: A Use Case Driven Approach*
ISBN 0-201-54435-0

Ivar Jacobson, Martin Griss, and Patrik Jonsson,
Software Reuse: Architecture, Process and Organization for Business Success
ISBN 0-201-92476-5

David Jordan, *C++ Object Databases: Programming with the ODMG Standard*
ISBN 0-201-63488-0

Wilf LaLonde, *Discovering Smalltalk*
ISBN 0-8053-2720-7

Lockheed Martin Advanced Concepts Center and Rational Software Corporation, *Succeeding with the Booch and OMT Methods: A Practical Approach*
ISBN 0-8053-2279-5

Thomas Mowbray and William Ruh, *Inside CORBA: Distributed Object Standards and Applications*
ISBN 0-201-89540-4

Ira Pohl, *Object-Oriented Programming Using C++, Second Edition*
ISBN 0-201-89550-1

Terry Quatrani, *Visual Modeling with Rational Rose and UML*
ISBN 0-201-61016-3

Yen-Ping Shan and Ralph H. Earle, *Enterprise Computing with Objects: From Client/Server Environments to the Internet*
ISBN 0-201-32566-7

David N. Smith, *IBM Smalltalk: The Language*
ISBN 0-8053-0908-X

Daniel Tkach, Walter Fang, and Andrew So, *Visual Modeling Technique: Object Technology Using Visual Programming*
ISBN 0-8053-2574-3

Daniel Tkach and Richard Puttick, *Object Technology in Application Development, Second Edition*
ISBN 0-201-49833-2

Available Summer/Fall 1998

Grady Booch, James Rumbaugh, and Ivar Jacobson,
Unified Modeling Language User Guide
ISBN 0-201-57168-4

Ivar Jacobson, Grady Booch, and James Rumbaugh,
The Objectory Software Development Process
ISBN 0-201-57169-2

James Rumbaugh, Ivar Jacobson, and Grady Booch,
Unified Modeling Language Reference Manual
ISBN 0-201-30998-X

VISUAL MODELING WITH RATIONAL ROSE AND UML

TERRY QUATRANI

ADDISON-WESLEY

An imprint of Addison Wesley Longman, Inc.
Reading, Massachusetts • Harlow, England
Menlo Park, California • Berkeley, California
Don Mills, Ontario • Sydney • Bonn
Amsterdam • Tokyo • Mexico City

TO MY HUSBAND, ERNIE,
AND MY SONS, MIKE, MATT, AND STEVE,
FOR THEIR LOVE, PATIENCE, AND SUPPORT
AS MOM SPENT YET ANOTHER NIGHT
IN FRONT OF HER COMPUTER

Many of the designations used by manufacturers and sellers to distinguish their products are claimed as trademarks. Where those designations appear in this book, and Addison-Wesley was aware of a trademark claim, the designations have been printed in initial caps or all caps.

The author and publishers have taken care in the preparation of this book, but make no expressed or implied warranty of any kind and assume no responsibility for errors or omissions. No liability is assumed for incidental or consequential damages in connection with or arising out of the use of the information or programs contained herein.

The publisher offers discounts on this book when ordered in quantity for special sales. For more information, please contact: Corporate & Professional Publishing Group, Addison Wesley Longman, Inc., One Jacob Way, Reading, Massachusetts 01867

Library of Congress Cataloging-in-Publication Data
Quatrani, Terry.
    Visual modeling with rational rose and UML / Terry Quatrani.
        p.   cm.
    Includes bibliographical references and index.
    ISBN 0-201-31016-3 (alk. paper)
    1. Visual programming (Computer science)   2. Object-oriented methods (Computer science)   3. UML (Computer science)   I. Title.
    QA78.64.Q38 1998
    005.1'17—dc21   97-45825
                                                                              CIP

Printed in the United States of America. Printed simultaneously in Canada.

ISBN 0-201-31016-3
Text printed on recycled and acid-free paper.
3 4 5 6 7 8 MA   01 00 99 98

3rd Printing April, 1998

Contents

CHAPTER 7

CHAPTER 8

CHAPTER 9

Foreword

EDWARD TUFTE, in his seminal work, *The Visual Display of Quantitative Information,* notes that "graphics reveal data." What he means by this statement is that certain complex sets of data, when visualized graphically, convey far more information to the reader than the raw data itself. So it is with software; as our industry moves to develop systems of greater and greater complexity, our ability to manage that complexity follows our ability to visualize our systems above the level of their raw lines of code. Indeed, the market success of languages such as Visual Basic (for which there are more developers than any other programming language, even COBOL), and visual front ends to C++ and Java point out that visualization is essential to the development of complex systems. With the advent of distributed and concurrent systems of all kinds, and especially of web-based systems, the need for visualization of software has never been greater.

As Terry Quatrani writes, her book is "an introduction to the concepts needed to visualize a software system—a process, a notation and a modeling tool." As I look back over the last several years, it's clear that these three key components of software development have matured and multiplied tremendously. Developers now have a wide range of tools to assist in every aspect of the software development process. Furthermore, standards in methods, languages, and tools, have begun to emerge, allowing the industry to focus cycle time on actually developing and deploying complex software systems, rather than being distracted by the so-called method wars and language wars. I have been privileged to participate in this process of standardization, most recently in the development of the Unified Modeling Language (UML). It's been gratifying to see the widespread industry support and acceptance of the UML and the growing popularity of Rational Rose and the Rational Objectory Process. As our industry faces the challenges of building large-scale distributed object applications, the use of common tools and methods and industry-wide standards offer the promise of achieving the true interoperability and reuse of software long sought.

Terry has been working with Rational Rose and the UML almost from its inception. Her knowledge and experience of methods is extensive, and she has been a driving force in the training and mentoring of Rational's customers on the use of the UML. This book is an extension of her everyday work and clearly reflects her pragmatic knowledge of these subjects and the insights that she has gained from working on a multitude of complex software systems. Developers seeking guidance in visualizing a software system will learn from Terry how to specify, visualize, document, and create a software solution using the industry's leading tools and methods, all expressed in standard notation. I've enjoyed the benefits of Terry's experience and insight for years; I know you will too.

Grady Booch

Preface

GOALS

FOLLOWING MARTIN FOWLER'S style in his book *UML Distilled,* let me tell you what this book is *not.*

- It is not a tutorial on all the ins and outs of analysis and design using UML. This is the purpose of the Unified Modeling Language User Guide being developed by Grady Booch (with help from the other amigos).

- It is not a tutorial on all the details in the Rational Objectory Process. This is the purpose of the Objectory Software Development Process being developed by Ivar Jacobson (with help from the other amigos).

- It is not an explanation of all the notation and semantics of the UML. This is the purpose of the Unified Modeling Language Reference Manual being developed by Jim Rumbaugh (with help from the other amigos).

- It is not an abridged explanation of the UML Notation, which is very nicely done in Martin Fowler's book.

- It is not a book on software architecture or C++ design; many books and papers are available on these subjects.

Well then, what is it? This book is an introduction to the concepts needed to visualize a software system—a process, a notation, and a tool. It provides practical guidance on visual modeling, using a limited version of the Rational Objectory Process, the Unified Modeling Language (UML), and the Rational Rose tool. It demonstrates how all three elements (process, notation, and tool) can be used in tandem to specify, visualize, document, and create a software solution to a problem in an iterative and incremental manner.

APPROACH

THIS BOOK TAKES a practical approach to teaching visual modeling techniques and the UML. It uses a case study to show the analysis and design of an application. The application is a course registration system for a university. This problem domain was chosen because it is easily understood and is not specific to any field of computer science. The reader can concentrate on the specifics of modeling the domain rather than investing time in understanding an unfamiliar problem domain.

The problem is treated seriously enough to give the reader practical exercise with visual modeling techniques and the feeling for solving a real problem, without being so realistic that the reader is bogged down in details. Thus, many interesting and perhaps necessary requirements, considerations, and constraints were put aside to produce a simplified, yet useful case study fitting the scope of this book.

For additional details on visual modeling and the UML, or on applying the techniques to your application, you should consider the training and mentoring services offered by Rational Software Corporation. Rational Software Corporation may be contacted at 2800 San Tomas Expressway, Santa Clara, CA 95051, 1-800-767-3237. You may send e-mail to Rational Software Corporation at product_info@rational.com. You can also visit the Rational website at www.rational.com.

CHAPTER SUMMARIES

Chapter 1: Introduction
Introduces the techniques, language, and process used throughout the book. This chapter discusses the benefits of visual modeling, the history of the UML, and the software development process used.

Chapter 2: Beginning a Project
Contains information that is related to the Course Registration System case study that is used throughout the book.

Chapter 3: Creating Use Cases

Discusses the techniques used to examine system behavior from a use case approach.

Chapter 4: Finding Classes

Discusses the concepts and notations used for finding objects and classes. This chapter also discusses the UML concepts of stereotypes and packages.

Chapter 5: Discovering Object Interaction

Discusses the addition of scenarios to the system to describe how use cases are realized as interactions among societies of objects. This chapter also examines how sequence diagrams and collaboration diagrams may be used to capture scenarios.

Chapter 6: Specifying Relationships

Illustrates the definition of relationships between classes in the system. Specifically, the concepts of association and aggregation are explored.

Chapter 7: Adding Behavior and Structure

Shows how the needed structure and behavior of classes are added to the model under development.

Chapter 8: Discovering Inheritance

Illustrates the application of generalization and specialization principles to discover superclass/subclass relationships.

Chapter 9: Analyzing Object Behavior

Uses Harel state transition diagrams to provide additional analysis techniques for classes with significant dynamic behavior.

Chapter 10: Checking the Model

Discusses techniques used to blend and check models for consistency. These techniques are needed when different teams are working on a single project in parallel.

Chapter 11: Designing the System Architecture

Contains an introduction to the concepts and notation needed to specify and document the system architecture. This chapter is not meant to be a tell-all process guide to the development of the architecture—it is meant to be a guide to the notation and process used to specify, visualize, and document the system architecture. It is placed at this point in the structure of the book since the architectural decisions specified in this chapter must be made prior to the information given after this chapter.

Chapter 12: Building the Iterations

Discusses the iteration planning process. This chapter also looks at the UML notation used to specify and document the design decisions that occur during the implementation of an iteration. It does not focus on good (or bad) design decisions, but at the process and notations used to capture the design of an iteration.

Appendix A

Provides step-by-step guides to code generation and reverse engineering using the *Rational Rose / C+ +* tool. Future appendixes will be available at the Addison-Wesley website for step-by step guides to the other variants of Rational Rose.

Appendix B

Provides sample code generated by Rational Rose/C+ +.

Glossary

Provides definitions of terms used throughout the book.

ACKNOWLEDGMENTS

I WOULD LIKE to thank a number of individuals for their contributions to the content, style, presentation, and writing of this book.

Special thanks to the following people:

Steve Bailey (Tier Technologies), Alex Baran, Kurt Bittner, Grady Booch, Jim Conallen, Ed Delio, Matt Drahzal, Maria Ericsson,

Jim Ford, Adam Frankl, Scott Frohman, Jim Gillespie, Dorothy
Green, Jon Hopkins, Ivar Jacobson, Jason James, Philippe Kruchten,
Eric Lipanovich, Peter Luckey, Greg Meyers, Sue Mickel,
Laura Mullins, Larry O'Brien, Sylvia Pacheco, Hugo Sanchez,
Charlie Snyder, Lynne Steele, Walker Royce, Jim Rumbaugh,
Tom Schultz, John Smith, and Dave Tropeano. I would also like
to thank my editor Carter Shanklin and his assistant Rachel Beavers,
for without their help this book would never have gone to print.

Chapter 1

Introduction

WHAT IS VISUAL MODELING?

VISUAL MODELING IS a way of thinking about problems using models organized around real-world ideas. Models are useful for understanding problems, communicating with everyone involved with the project (customers, domain experts, analysts, designers, etc.), modeling enterprises, preparing documentation, and designing programs and databases. Modeling promotes better understanding of requirements, cleaner designs, and more maintainable systems.

Models are abstractions that portray the essentials of a complex problem or structure by filtering out nonessential details, thus making the problem easier to understand. Abstraction is a fundamental human capability that permits us to deal with complexity. Engineers, artists, and craftsmen have built models for thousands of years to try out designs before executing them. Development of software systems should be no exception. To build complex systems, the developer must abstract different views of the system, build models using precise notations, verify that the models satisfy the requirements of the system, and gradually add detail to transform the models into an implementation.

We build models of complex systems because we cannot comprehend such systems in their entirety. There are limits to the human capacity to understand complexity. This concept may be seen in the world of architecture. If you want to build a shed in your backyard, you may just start building; if you want to build a new house, you probably need a blueprint; if you are building a skyscraper, you definitely need a blueprint. The same is true in the world of software. Staring at lines of source code or even analyzing forms in Visual Basic does little to provide the programmer with a global view of a development project. Constructing a model allows the designer to focus on the big picture of how a project's components interact, without having to get bogged down in the specific details of each component.

Increasing complexity, resulting from a highly competitive and ever-changing business environment, offers unique challenges to system developers. Models help us organize, visualize, understand,

and create complex things. They are used to help us meet the challenges of developing software today and into the future.

THE TRIANGLE FOR SUCCESS

I HAVE OFTEN used the triangle for success as shown in Figure 1-1 to explain the components needed for a successful project. You need all three facets—a notation, a process, and a tool. You can learn a notation, but if you don't know how to use it (process), you will probably fail. You may have a great process, but if you can't communicate the process (notation), you will probably fail. And lastly, if you cannot document the artifacts of your work (tool), you will probably fail.

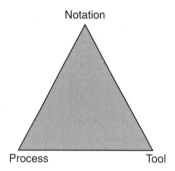

Figure 1-1   Triangle for Success

THE ROLE OF NOTATION

NOTATION PLAYS AN important part in any model—it is the glue that holds the process together. "Notation has three roles:

- It serves as the language for communicating decisions that are not obvious or cannot be inferred from the code itself.
- It provides semantics that are rich enough to capture all important strategic and tactical decisions.

- It offers a form concrete enough for humans to reason and for tools to manipulate."[1]

The Unified Modeling Language (UML) provides a very robust notation, which grows from analysis into design. Certain elements of the notation (for example, classes, associations, aggregations, inheritance) are introduced during analysis. Other elements of the notation (for example, containment implementation indicators and properties) are introduced during design.

HISTORY OF THE UML

DURING THE NINETIES many different methodologies, along with their own set of notations, were introduced to the market. Three of the most popular methods were OMT (Rumbaugh), Booch, and OOSE (Jacobson). Each method had its own value and emphasis. OMT was strong in analysis and weaker in the design area. Booch 1991 was strong in design and weaker in analysis. Jacobson was strong in behavior analysis and weaker in the other areas.

As time moved on, Booch wrote his second book, which adopted a lot of the good analysis techniques advocated by Rumbaugh and Jacobson among others. Rumbaugh published a series of articles that have become known as OMT-2 that adopted a lot of the good design techniques of Booch. The methods were beginning to converge but they still had their own unique notations. The use of different notations brought confusion to the market since one symbol meant different things to different people. For example, a filled circle was a multiplicity indicator in OMT and an aggregation symbol in Booch. You will hear the term *method wars* being used to describe this period of time—is a class a cloud or a rectangle? Which one is better?

The end of the method wars as far as notation is concerned comes with the adoption of the Unified Modeling Language (UML). "UML is a language used to specify, visualize, and document the artifacts of an object-oriented system under development. It represents the unification of the Booch, OMT, and Objectory notations,

---

[1] Booch, Grady. *Object Solutions.* Redwood City, CA: Addison-Wesley, 1995.

as well as the best ideas from a number of other methodologists as shown in Figure 1-2. By unifying the notations used by these object-oriented methods, the Unified Modeling Language provides the basis for a *de facto* standard in the domain of object-oriented analysis and design founded on a wide base of user experience."[2]

The UML is an attempt to standardize the artifacts of analysis and design: semantic models, syntactic notation, and diagrams. The first public draft (version 0.8) was introduced in October 1995. Feedback from the public and Ivar Jacobson's input were included in the next two versions (0.9 in July 1996 and 0.91 in October 1996). Version 1.0 was presented to the Object Management Group (OMG) for standardization in July 1997.

Additional enhancements were incorporated into the 1.1 version of UML, which was presented to the OMG in September 1997.

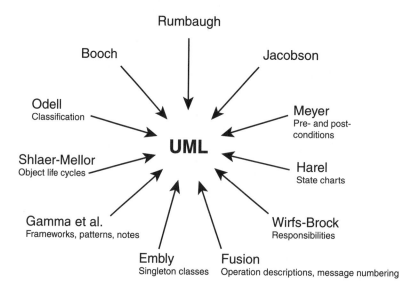

Figure 1-2   UML Inputs

---

[2] *The Unified Method,* Draft Edition (0.8). Rational Software Corporation, October 1995.

THE ROLE OF PROCESS

A SUCCESSFUL DEVELOPMENT project satisfies or exceeds the customer's expectations, is developed in a timely and economical fashion, and is resilient to change and adaptation. The development life cycle must promote creativity and innovation. At the same time, the development process must be controlled and measured to ensure that the project is indeed completed. "Creativity is essential to the crafting of all well-structured object-oriented architectures, but developers allowed completely unrestrained creativity tend to never reach closure. Similarly, discipline is required when organizing the efforts of a team of developers, but too much discipline gives birth to an ugly bureaucracy that kills all attempts at innovation."[3] A well-managed iterative and incremental life cycle provides the necessary control without affecting creativity.

WHAT IS ITERATIVE AND INCREMENTAL DEVELOPMENT?

IN AN ITERATIVE and incremental life cycle (Figure 1-3), development proceeds as a series of iterations that evolve into the final system. Each iteration consists of one or more of the following process components: requirements capture, analysis, design, implementation, and test. The developers do not assume that all requirements are known at the beginning of the life cycle; indeed change is anticipated throughout all phases.

This type of life cycle is a risk-mitigating process. Technical risks are assessed and prioritized early in the life cycle and are revised during the development of each iteration. Risks are attached to each iteration so that successful completion of the iteration alleviates the risks attached to it. The releases are scheduled to ensure that the highest risks are tackled first. Building the system in this fashion exposes and mitigates the risks of the system early in the

---

[3] Booch, Grady. *Object Solutions*. Redwood City, CA: Addison-Wesley, 1995.

life cycle. The result of this life cycle approach is less risk coupled with minimal investment.[4]

Figure 1-3   Iterative and Incremental Development

THE RATIONAL OBJECTORY PROCESS

CONTROL FOR AN iterative and incremental life cycle is supported by employing the Rational Objectory Process—an extensive set of guidelines that address the technical and organizational aspects of software development focusing on requirements analysis and design.[5]

The Rational Objectory Process is structured along two dimensions:

- Time—division of the life cycle into phases and iterations
- Process components—production of a specific set of artifacts with well-defined activities

---

[4] More information on the application of an iterative and incremental approach to software development may be found in the article "A Rational Development Process" by Philippe Kruchten, *CrossTalk,* 9(7), July 1996, pp. 11–16. This paper is also available on the Rational website: http://www.rational.com.

[5] Rational Software Corporation. *The Objectory Process—Introduction,* 1996. Information may be found on the Rational website: www.rational.com.

Both dimensions must be taken into account for a project to succeed.

Structuring a project along the time dimension involves the adoption of the following time-based phases:

- Inception—specifying the project vision

- Elaboration—planning the necessary activities and required resources; specifying the features and designing the architecture

- Construction—building the product as a series of incremental iterations

- Transition—supplying the product to the user community (manufacturing, delivering, and training)

Structuring the project along the process component dimension includes the following activities:

- Requirements capture—a narration of what the system should do

- Analysis and design—a description of how the system will be realized in the implementation phase

- Implementation—the production of the code that will result in an executable system

- Test—the verification of the entire system

Figure 1-4 shows how the process components are applied to each time-based phase.

Each activity of the process component dimension typically is applied to each phase of time-based dimension. However, the degree to which a particular process component is applied is dependent upon the phase of development. For example, you may decide to do a proof of concept prototype during the Inception Phase, and thus, you will be doing more than just requirements capture (you will be doing the analysis, design, implementation, and test needed to complete the prototype). The majority of the analysis process component occurs during the Elaboration Phase. However, it is also advisable to complete the first few iterations of the system during this phase. These first few iterations typically are used to validate the analysis decisions made for the architecture of the system.

Figure 1-4   The Development Process

Hence, you are doing more than just analyzing the problem. During the Construction Phase of development, the system is completed as a series of iterations. As with any type of development structure, things always crop up as the system is built; thus, you are still doing some analysis.

The diagram is meant to be a guideline for the life cycle of your project. The main point is if you are still trying to figure out what you are supposed to be building as you are writing the code, you are probably in trouble. You should also note that testing is applied throughout the iteration process—you do not wait until all the code is done to see if it all works together!

This book uses a simplified version of the Rational Objectory Process, and concentrates on the use of the UML to capture and document the decisions made during the Inception and Elaboration Phases of development. The last few chapters lightly cover construction of the system. Although testing is a very integral part of system development, it is beyond the scope of this book.

THE RATIONAL ROSE TOOL

ANY SOFTWARE DEVELOPMENT method is best supported by a tool. When I first started OO modeling, my tool was paper and a pencil, which left a lot to be desired. There are many tools on the market today—everything from simple drawing tools to sophisticated object modeling tools. This book makes use of the tool Rational Rose. At every step, there is a description of how to use the tool to complete the step. Although this book uses the 4.0 version of Rational Rose, the same steps may be applied to later versions of the tool.

The Rational Rose product family is designed to provide the software developer with a complete set of visual modeling tools for development of robust, efficient solutions to real business needs in the client/server, distributed enterprise, and real-time systems environments. Rational Rose products share a common universal standard, making modeling accessible to nonprogrammers wanting to model business processes as well as to programmers modeling applications logic. A demo version of the Rational Rose tool may be obtained at the Rational Software Corporation website at www.rational.com.

Although this book uses the Rational Rose tool, a subset of the diagrams are available in the Microsoft Visual Modeler tool. Microsoft Visual Modeler is the entry-level product, designed specifically for the first-time modeler. The tool provides the capability to:

- Identify and design business objects, and then map them to software components
- Partition services across a three-tiered service model
- Design how components will be distributed across a network
- Generate Visual Basic code frameworks directly from your model
- Use reverse engineering to create models from existing components and applications
- Use round-trip engineering facilities to keep your designs synchronized with your code

Rational Rose/Visual Basic extends Visual Modeler for dynamic behaviors, such as business requirements analysis, business scenario analysis with sequence and collaboration diagrams, state modeling, additional code generation capabilities for DDL and IDL, along with the inclusion of a scripting language to provide access to the Rose domain.

SUMMARY

VISUAL MODELING IS a way of thinking about problems using models organized around real-world ideas. Models are useful for understanding problems, communication, modeling enterprises, preparing documentation, and designing programs and databases. Modeling promotes better understanding of requirements, cleaner designs, and more maintainable systems. Notation plays an important part in any model—it is the glue that holds the process together. The Unified Modeling Language (UML) provides a very robust notation, which grows from analysis into design.

A successful development project satisfies or exceeds the customer's expectations, is developed in a timely and economical fashion, and is resilient to change and adaptation. The development life cycle must promote creativity and innovation. A well-managed iterative and incremental life cycle provides the necessary control without affecting creativity. In an iterative and incremental development life cycle, development proceeds as a series of iterations that evolve into the final system. Each iteration consists of one or more of the following process components: requirements analysis, analysis, design, implementation, and test.

Control for an iterative and incremental life cycle is provided in the Rational Objectory Process—an extensive set of guidelines that address the technical and organizational aspects of software development, focusing on requirements analysis and design. This book uses a simplified version of the Rational Objectory Process.

The Rational Rose product family is designed to provide the software developer with a complete set of visual modeling tools for development of robust, efficient solutions to real business needs in the client/server, distributed enterprise, and real-time systems environments.

Chapter 2

Beginning a Project

DEFINING THE RIGHT PROJECT

THE MOST IMPORTANT question to ask when developing a system is not a methodological question. It is not a technical question. It is a seemingly simple, yet remarkably difficult question: "Is this the right system to make?" Unfortunately, this question is often never asked nor answered. Although misguided methodology or technically tough problems can cause projects to fail, sufficient resources and heroic effort by talented people often can save them. But nothing can save a system that is not needed or that automates the wrong thing.

Before starting a project, there must be an idea for it. The process of coming up with an idea for a system along with a general idea of its requirements and form occurs during the Inception Phase. It finishes the statement: "The system we want does. . . ." During this phase of development, a vision for the idea is established, and many assumptions are either validated or rejected. Activities that occur involve the solicitation of ideas, the preliminary identification of risks, the identification of external interfaces, the identification of the major functionality that must be provided by the system, and possibly some "proof of concept" prototypes. Ideas come from many sources: customers, domain experts, other developers, industry experts, feasibility studies, and review of existing systems. It is important to note that any prototyping done during this phase should be considered throw-away code since the code generated is merely to support a list of assumptions and has not been fully analyzed or designed.

The process used during this phase of development can be done formally or informally, but it always involves considering the business needs, the available resources, the possible technology, and the user community desires, along with several ideas for new systems. Brainstorming, research, trade studies, cost-benefit analysis, use case analysis, and prototyping can then be performed to produce the target system's concept along with defined purposes, priorities, and context. Usually, a first-pass cut at resource and schedule planning is also done during this phase. For some projects, the product vision can be sketched on the back of a napkin. For others, the product vision may be a formal phase that is iteratively performed until enough level of detail of the target system has been specified.

An adequate Inception Phase establishes the high-level requirements for a desirable and feasible system, both technologically and sociologically. An inadequate Inception Phase leads to systems so unwanted, expensive, impossible, and ill-defined that they are typically never finished or used.

EASTERN STATE UNIVERSITY (ESU) BACKGROUND

THE ESU COURSE registration problem will be used as an example throughout this book.

The process of assigning professors to courses and the registration of students is a frustrating and time-consuming experience.

After the professors of ESU have decided which courses they are going to teach for the semester, the Registrar's office enters the information into the computer system. A batch report is printed for the professors indicating which courses they will teach. A course catalog is printed and distributed to the students.

Currently, the students fill out (mulitpart, multicolor) registration forms that indicate their choice in courses, and return the completed forms to the Registrar's office. The typical student load is four courses. The staff of the Registrar's office then enters the students' forms into the mainframe computer system. Once the students' curriculum for the semester has been entered, a batch job is run overnight to assign students to courses. Most of the time the students get their first choice; however, in those cases where there is a conflict, the Registrar's office talks with each student to get additional choices. Once all the students have been successfully assigned to courses, a hard copy of the students' curriculum is sent to the students for their verification. Most student registrations are processed within a week, but some exceptional cases take up to two weeks to solve.

Once the initial registration period is completed, professors receive a student roster for each course they are scheduled to teach.

RISKS FOR THE COURSE REGISTRATION PROBLEM

THE DEVELOPMENT TEAM identified that the major risk to the system involved the ability to store and access the curriculum information efficiently. They developed several prototypes that evaluated data storage and access mechanisms for each database management system under consideration. The results of the prototypes led to the decision that the database risk could be mitigated. Additional prototypes were also developed to study the hardware needs for the university as a result of moving to an online registration system.

ESU COURSE REGISTRATION PROBLEM STATEMENT

AT THE BEGINNING of each semester, students may request a course catalog containing a list of course offerings needed for the semester. Information about each course, such as professor, department, and prerequisites are included to help students make informed decisions.

The new system will allow students to select four course offerings for the coming semester. In addition, each student will indicate two alternative choices in case a course offering becomes filled or canceled. No course offering will have more than ten students or fewer than three students. A course offering with fewer than three students will be canceled. Once the registration process is completed for a student, the registration system sends information to the billing system so the student can be billed for the semester.

Professors must be able to access the online system to indicate which courses they will be teaching, and to see which students signed up for their course offerings.

For each semester, there is a period of time that students can change their schedule. Students must be able to access the system during this time to add or drop courses.

SUMMARY

THE INCEPTION PHASE is a discovery phase. The problem to be solved is verbalized and discussed among the team and with customers. Assumptions are expressed and may be verified or rejected using proof of concept prototyping techniques. The output of this phase is the identification of the external interfaces, an initial risk assessment, and a set of system requirements. Customers, clients, users, and other interested parties bring various ideas and points of view to this phase and offer the possibility of an early and enthusiastic buy-in.

Chapter 3

Creating Use Cases

SYSTEM BEHAVIOR

THE BEHAVIOR OF the system under development, that is what
functionality must be provided by the system, is documented in
a use case model that illustrates the system's intended functions
(use cases), its surroundings (actors), and relationships between the
use cases and actors (use case diagrams). The most important role
of a use case model is one of communication. It provides a vehicle
used by the customers or end users and the developers to discuss
the system's functionality and behavior.

The use case model starts in the Inception Phase with the
identification of actors and principal use cases for the system.
The model is then matured in the Elaboration Phase—more detailed
information is added to the identified use cases, and additional use
cases are added on an as-needed basis.

ACTORS

ACTORS ARE NOT part of the system—they represent anyone or anything that must interact with the system. An actor may

- Only input information to the system
- Only receive information from the system
- Input and receive information to and from the system

Typically, these actors are found in the problem statement and
by conversations with customers and domain experts. The following
questions may be used to help identify the actors for a system:

- Who is interested in a certain requirement?
- Where in the organization is the system used?
- Who will benefit from the use of the system?
- Who will supply the system with this information,
  use this information, and remove this information?
- Who will support and maintain the system?

- Does the system use an external resource?
- Does one person play several different roles?
- Do several people play the same role?
- Does the system interact with a legacy system?

In the UML, an actor is represented as a stickman, as shown in Figure 3-1.

Figure 3-1   UML Notation for an Actor

What Constitutes a Good Actor?

Care must be taken when identifying the actors for a system. This identification is done in an iterative fashion—the first cut at the list of actors for a system is rarely the final list. For example, is a new student a different actor than a returning student? Suppose you initially say the answer to this question is yes. The next step is to identify how the actor interacts with the system. If the new student uses the system differently than the returning student, they are different actors. If they use the system the same way, they are the same actor.

Another example is the creation of an actor for every role a person may play. This may also be overkill. A good example is a teaching assistant in the ESU Course Registration System. The teaching assistant takes classes and teaches classes. The capabilities needed to select courses to take and to select courses to teach is already captured by the identification of functionality needed by the Student and the Professor actors. Therefore, there is no need for a Teaching Assistant actor.

By looking at the identified actors and documenting how they use the system, you will iteratively arrive at a good set of actors for the system.

Actors in the ESU Course Registration System

The previous questions were answered as follows:

- Students want to register for courses

- Professors want to select courses to teach

- The Registrar must create the curriculum and generate a catalog for the semester

- The Registrar must maintain all the information about courses, professors, and students

- The Billing System must receive billing information from the system

Based on the answers to the questions posed, the following actors have been identified: Student, Professor, Registrar, and the Billing System.

CREATING ACTORS IN RATIONAL ROSE

1. Right-click on the Use Case View package in the browser to make the shortcut menu visible.
2. Select the New:Actor menu option. A new actor called New Class is placed in the browser.
3. With the actor called New Class selected, enter the desired name of the actor.

The Browser view of the actors for the ESU Course Registration System is shown in Figure 3-2.

Actor Documentation

A brief description for each actor should be added to the model. The description should identify the role the actor plays while interacting with the system.

The actor descriptions for the ESU Course Registration System are:

Figure 3-2   Actors

- **Student**—a person who is registered to take classes at the University

- **Professor**—a person who is certified to teach classes at the University

- **Registrar**—the person who is responsible for the maintenance of the ESU Course Registration System

- **Billing System**—the external system responsible for student billing

DOCUMENTING ACTORS IN RATIONAL ROSE

1. If the documentation window is not visible, open the documentation window by selecting the Documentation menu choice from the View menu.
2. Click to select the Actor in the browser.
3. Position the cursor in the documentation window and enter the documentation.

The documentation for the Student actor is shown in Figure 3-3.

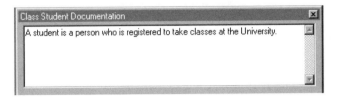

Figure 3-3   Student Actor Documentation

USE CASES

USE CASES MODEL a dialogue between an actor and the system. They represent the functionality provided by the system; that is, what capabilities will be provided to an actor by the system. The collection of use cases for a system constitute all the defined ways the system may be used. The formal definition for a use case is: A use case is a sequence of transactions performed by a system that yields a measurable result of values for a particular actor.

The following questions may be used to help identify the use cases for a system:

- What are the tasks of each actor?

- Will any actor create, store, change, remove, or read information in the system?

- What use cases will create, store, change, remove, or read this information?

- Will any actor need to inform the system about sudden, external changes?

- Does any actor need to be informed about certain occurrences in the system?

- What use cases will support and maintain the system?

- Can all functional requirements be performed by the use cases?

In the UML, a use case is represented as an oval, as shown in Figure 3-4.

Figure 3-4   UML Notation for a Use Case

What Constitutes a Good Use Case?

Over the years there has been a lot of discussion dealing with the "goodness" of a use case. One problem that I have encountered is the level of detail found in use cases. That is, how big (or how little) should they be? There is no one, right answer. The rule of thumb that I apply is:

> A use case typically represents a major piece of functionality that is complete from beginning to end. A use case must deliver something of value to an actor.

For example, in the ESU Course Registration System, the student must select the courses for a semester, the student must be added to the course offerings, and the student must be billed. Is this three use cases, or just one? I would make it one since the functionality represents what happens from beginning to end. What good would the system be if a student was not added to the courses selected (or at least notified if the addition does not occur)? Or if the student was not billed (the University would not stay in business if all courses were free!)?

Another problem is how to bundle functionality that is different but seems to belong together. For example, the Registrar must add courses, delete courses, and modify courses. Three use cases, or one use case? Here again, I would make one use case—the maintenance of the curriculum, since the functionality is started by the same actor (the Registrar) and deals with the same entities in the system (the curriculum).

Use Cases in the ESU Course Registration System

The following needs must be addressed by the system:

- The Student actor needs to use the system to register for courses
- After the course selection process is completed, the Billing System must be supplied with billing information
- The Professor actor needs to use the system to select the courses to teach for a semester, and must be able to receive a course roster from the system
- The Registrar is responsible for the generation of the course catalog for a semester, and for the maintenance of all information about the curriculum, the students, and the professors needed by the system

Based on these needs, the following use cases have been identified:

- Register for courses
- Select courses to teach
- Request course roster
- Maintain course information
- Maintain professor information
- Maintain student information
- Create course catalog

CREATING USE CASES IN RATIONAL ROSE

1. Right-click on the Use Case View in the browser to make the shortcut menu visible.
2. Select the New:Use Case menu option. A new unnamed use case is placed in the browser.
3. With the use case selected, enter the desired name of the use case.

The browser view of the use cases for the ESU Course Registration System is shown in Figure 3-5.

Figure 3-5   Use Cases

Brief Description of a Use Case

The brief description of a use case states the purpose of the use case in a few sentences, providing a high-level definition of the functionality provided by the use case. This description is typically created during the Inception Phase as the use case is identified.

The brief description of the *Register for Courses* use case is:

> This use case is started by the Student. It provides the capability to create, delete, modify, and/or review a student schedule for a specified semester.

CREATING A USE CASE BRIEF DESCRIPTION IN RATIONAL ROSE

1. Click to select the use case in the browser.
2. Position the cursor in the documentation window and enter the brief description for the use case. If the documentation window is not visible, select the View:Documentation menu choice to make the window visible.

The brief description of the *Register for Courses* use case is shown in Figure 3-6.

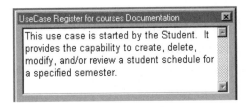

Figure 3-6   Use Case Brief Description

The Flow of Events for a Use Case

Each use case also is documented with a flow of events. The flow of events for a use case is a description of the events needed to accomplish the required behavior of the use case. The flow of events is written in terms of what the system should do, not how the system does it. That is, it is written in the language of the domain, not in terms of implementation. The flow of events should include:

- When and how the use case starts and ends
- What interaction the use case has with the actors
- What data is needed by the use case
- The normal sequence of events for the use case
- The description of any alternate or exceptional flows

The flow of events documentation typically is created in the Elaboration Phase in an iterative manner. At first, only a brief description of the steps needed to carry out the normal flow of the use case (i.e., what functionality is provided by the use case) is written. As analysis progresses, the steps are fleshed out to add more detail. Finally, the exceptional flows are added to the use case (the what happens if . . . part of the flow of events).

Each project should use a standard template for the creation of the flow of events document. I have found the following template to be useful.

X Flow of Events for the < name > Use Case

X.1 Preconditions

X.2 Main Flow

X.3 Subflows (if applicable)

X.4 Alternative Flows

where X is a number from 1 to the number of use cases.

A sample completed Flow of Events document for the *Select Courses to Teach* use case follows.

1.0 *Flow of Events for the* Select Courses to Teach *Use Case*

1.1 *Preconditions*

The Create Course Offerings *subflow of the* Maintain Courses *use case must execute before this use case begins.*

1.2 *Main Flow*

This use case begins when the professor logs onto the Registration System and enters his/her password. The system verifies that the password is valid (E-1) and prompts the professor to select the current semester or a future semester (E-2). The professor enters the desired semester. The system prompts the professor to select the desired activity: ADD, DELETE, REVIEW, PRINT, or QUIT.

If the activity selected is ADD, the S-1: Add a Course Offering *subflow is performed.*

If the activity selected is DELETE, the S-2: Delete a Course Offering *subflow is performed.*

If the activity selected is REVIEW, the S-3: Review Schedule *subflow is performed.*

If the activity selected is PRINT, the S-4: Print a Schedule *subflow is performed.*

If the activity selected is QUIT, the use case ends.

1.3 Subflows

S-1: Add a Course Offering
The system displays the course screen containing a field for a course name and number. The professor enters the name and number of a course (E-3). The system displays the course offerings for the entered course (E-4). The professor selects a course offering. The system links the professor to the selected course offering (E-5). The use case then begins again.

S-2: Delete a Course Offering
The system displays the course offering screen containing a field for a course offering name and number. The professor enters the name and number of a course offering (E-6). The system removes the link to the professor (E-7). The use case then begins again.

S-3: Review a Schedule
The system retrieves (E-8) and displays the following information for all course offerings for which the professor is assigned: course name, course number, course offering number, days of the week, time, and location. When the professor indicates that he/she is through reviewing, the use case begins again.

S-4: Print a Schedule
The system prints the professor schedule (E-9). The use case begins again.

1.4 Alternative Flows

E-1: An invalid professor ID number is entered. The user can re-enter a professor id number or terminate the use case.

E-2: An invalid semester is entered. The user can re-enter the semester or terminate the use case.

E-3: An invalid course name/number is entered. The user can re-enter a valid name/number combination or terminate the use case.

E-4: Course offerings cannot be displayed. The user is informed that this option is not available at the current time. The use case begins again.

E-5: A link between the professor and the course offering cannot be created. The information is saved and the system will create the link at a later time. The use case continues.

E-6: An invalid course offering name/number is entered. The user can re-enter a valid course offering name/number combination or terminate the use case.

E-7: A link between the professor and the course offering cannot be removed. The information is saved and the system will remove the link at a later time. The use case continues.

E-8: The system cannot retrieve schedule information. The use case then begins again.

E-9: The schedule cannot be printed. The user is informed that this option is not available at the current time. The use case begins again.

Use case flow of events documents are entered and maintained in documents external to Rational Rose. The documents are linked to the use case.

**LINKING FLOW OF EVENTS DOCUMENTS
TO USE CASES IN RATIONAL ROSE**

1. Right-click on the use case in the browser to make the shortcut menu visible.
2. Select the Specification menu option.
3. Select the Files tab.
4. Right-click to make the shortcut menu visible.
5. Select the Insert File menu option.
6. Browse to the appropriate directory and select the desired file.
7. Click the Open button.
8. Click the OK button to close the specification.

A linked use case flow of events document is shown in Figure 3-7.

USE CASE RELATIONSHIPS

AN ASSOCIATION RELATIONSHIP may exist between an actor and a use case. This type of association is often referred to as a *communicates association* since it represents communication between an actor and

Figure 3-7   Linked Flow of Events Document

a use case. An association may be navigable in both directions (actor to use case and use case to actor), or it may be navigable in only one direction (actor to use case or use case to actor). The navigation direction of an association represents who is initiating the communication (i.e., the actor is initiating the communication with the use case, the use case is initiating the communication with the actor). An association is represented as a line connecting the related elements. Navigation in only one direction is depicted by adding an arrowhead to the association line that denotes the direction.

There are two types of relationships that may exist between use cases: uses and extends. Multiple use cases may share pieces of the same functionality. This functionality is placed in a separate use case rather than documenting it in every use case that needs it. Uses relationships are created between the new use case and any other use case that uses its functionality. For example, each use case in the ESU Course Registration System starts with the verification of the user. This functionality can be captured in a User Verification use case, which is then used by other use cases as needed. A uses relationship is drawn as an arrow with a large hollow triangle (generalization arrow) at the end closest to the used use case.

An extends relationship is used to show:

- Optional behavior

- Behavior that is only run under certain conditions, such as triggering an alarm

- Several different flows which may be run based on actor selection

For example, a use case that monitors the flow of packages on a conveyer belt can be extended by a Trigger Alarm use case if the packages jam. At this time, no extensions have been identified for the ESU Course Registration System. An extends relationship is drawn as an arrow with a large hollow triangle (generalization arrow) at the end closest to the base use case.

The UML has a concept called a *stereotype,* which provides the capability of extending the basic modeling elements to create new elements. Thus, the concept of a stereotype allows the UML to have a minimal set of symbols that may be extended where needed to provide the communication artifacts that have meaning for the system under development. Stereotype names are included within guillemets (< < > >) and placed along the relationship line. Stereotypes are used to create the needed use case relationships. The stereotype < <communicates> > may be added to an association to show that the association is a communicates association. This is optional since an association is the only type of relationship allowed between an actor and a use case. Uses and extends relationships must use stereotypes since they are both represented by a generalization arrow.

Use case relationships are shown in Figure 3-8.

USE CASE DIAGRAMS

A USE CASE diagram is a graphical view of some or all of the actors, use cases, and their interactions identified for a system. Each system typically has a Main Use Case diagram, which is a picture of the

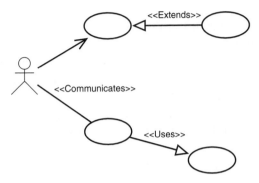

Figure 3-8   Use Case Relationships

system boundary (actors) and the major functionality provided by the system (use cases). Other use case diagrams may be created as needed. Some examples are:

- A diagram showing all the use cases for a selected actor
- A diagram showing all the use cases being implemented in an iteration
- A diagram showing a use case and all its relationships

CREATING THE MAIN USE CASE DIAGRAM IN RATIONAL ROSE

1. Double-click on the Main diagram in the Use Case View in the browser to open the diagram.
2. Click to select an actor in the browser and drag the actor onto the diagram.
3. Repeat step 2 for each additional actor needed in the diagram.
4. Click to select a use case in the browser and drag the use case onto the diagram.
5. Repeat step 4 for each additional use case needed in the diagram.

Note: Actors and use cases may also be created directly on a use case diagram by using the toolbar.

CREATING COMMUNICATES ASSOCIATIONS IN RATIONAL ROSE

1. Click to select the Association icon or the Unidirectional Association icon from the diagram toolbar. Note: If the Association icon is not present on the toolbar, it may be added by right-clicking on the toolbar, selecting the Customize menu choice from the shortcut menu, and adding the icon to the toolbar.

2. Click on an actor initiating a communication and drag the association line to the desired use case.

To add the Communicates stereotype (optional):

1. Double-click on the association line to make the Specification visible.

2. If this is the first time the stereotype is being used, enter Communicates in the Stereotype field. If a Communicates stereotype has already been created, click the arrow in the Stereotype field to make the drop-down menu visible and select Communicates.

3. Click the OK button to close the Specification.

4. Right-click on the association line to make the shortcut menu visible.

5. Select the Show Stereotype menu choice.

6. Repeat the preceding steps for each additional association relationship.

CREATING USES RELATIONSHIPS IN RATIONAL ROSE

1. Click to select the Generalization icon from the toolbar.

2. Click on the using use case and drag the Generalization icon to the used use case.

3. Double-click on the generalization arrow to make the Specification visible.

4. If this is the first time a uses relationship is being created, enter Uses in the Stereotype field. If a Uses stereotype has already been created, click the arrow in the Stereotype field to make the drop-down menu visible and select Uses.

5. Click the OK button to close the Specification.
6. Right-click on the generalization arrow to make the shortcut menu visible.
7. Select the Show Stereotype menu choice.

CREATING EXTENDS RELATIONSHIPS IN RATIONAL ROSE

1. Click to select the Generalization icon from the toolbar.
2. Click on the use case containing the extended functionality and drag the Generalization icon to the base use case.
3. Double-click on the generalization arrow to make the Specification visible.
4. If this is the first time an extends relationship is being created, enter Extends in the Stereotype field. If an Extends stereotype has already been created, click the arrow in the Stereotype field to make the drop-down menu visible and select Extends.
5. Click the OK button to close the Specification.
6. Right-click on the generalization arrow to make the shortcut menu visible.
7. Select the Show Stereotype menu choice.

The Main use case diagram for the ESU Course Registration System is shown in Figure 3-9.

CREATING ADDITIONAL USE CASE DIAGRAMS IN RATIONAL ROSE

1. Right-click on the Use Case View in the browser to make the shortcut menu visible.
2. Select the New:Use Case Diagram menu option.
3. While the use case diagram is selected, enter the name of the use case diagram.
4. Open the diagram and add actors, use cases, and inter-actions to the diagram as needed.

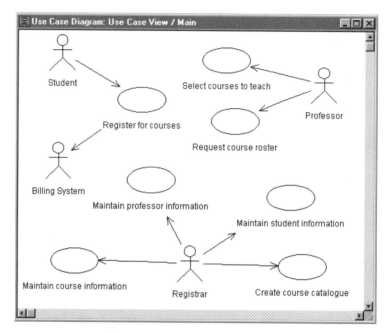

Figure 3-9   Main Use Case Diagram

An additional use case diagram is shown in Figure 3-10.

SUMMARY

SYSTEM BEHAVIOR IS documented in a use case model that illustrates the system's intended functions (use cases), its surroundings (actors), and the relationships between the use cases and actors (use case diagrams). The most important role of a use case model is to communicate the system's functionality and behavior to the customer or end user.

The use case model starts in the Inception Phase with the identification of the actors and the principal use cases for the system. The model is then matured in the Elaboration Phase.

Actors are not part of the system—they represent anyone or anything that must interact with the system under development. Use cases represent the functionality provided by the system. They model a dialogue between an actor and the system.

Figure 3-10   An Additional Use Case Diagram

Each use case contains a flow of events, which is a description of the events needed to accomplish the use case functionality. The flow of events is written in terms of what the system should do, not how the system does it. A use case diagram is a graphical representation of some or all of the actors, use cases, and their interactions for a system.

Two popular types of use case relationships are uses and extends. A uses relationship is drawn to show functionality that is shared by several use cases; an extends relationship depicts optional behavior of a use case.

Chapter 4

Finding Classes

WHAT IS AN OBJECT?

AN OBJECT IS a representation of an entity, either real-world or conceptual. An object can represent something concrete, such as Joe's truck or my computer, or a concept, such as a chemical process, a bank transaction, a purchase order, Mary's credit history, or an interest rate.

An object is a concept, abstraction, or thing with well-defined boundaries and meaning for an application. Each object in a system has three characteristics: state, behavior, and identity.

STATE, BEHAVIOR, AND IDENTITY

THE STATE OF an object is one of the possible conditions in which it may exist. The state of an object typically changes over time, and is defined by a set of properties (called attributes), with the values of the properties, plus the relationships the object may have with other objects. For example, a course offering object in the registration system may be in one of two states: *open* and *closed*. If the number of students registered for a course offering is less than 10, the state of the course offering is open. When the tenth student registers for the course offering, the state becomes closed.

Behavior determines how an object responds to requests from other objects, and typifies everything the object can do. Behavior is implemented by the set of operations for the object. In the registration system, a course offering could have the behaviors *add a student* and *delete a student*.

Identity means that each object is unique—even if its state is identical to that of another object. For example, Algebra 101, Section 1 and Algebra 101, Section 2 are two objects in the Course Registration System. Although they are both course offerings, they each have a unique identity.

In the UML, objects are represented as rectangles, and the name of the object is underlined as shown in Figure 4-1.

Algebra 101, Section 1

Figure 4-1   UML Notation for an Object

WHAT IS A CLASS?

A CLASS IS a description of a group of objects with common properties (attributes), common behavior (operations), common relationships to other objects, and common semantics. Thus, a class is a template to create objects. Each object is an instance of some class, and objects cannot be instances of more than one class. For example, the CourseOffering class may be defined with the following characteristics:

- Attributes—location, time offered
- Operations—retrieve location, retrieve time of day, add a student to the offering

Algebra 101, Section 1 and Algebra 101, Section 2 are objects belonging to the CourseOffering class. Each object would have a value for the attributes and access to the operations specified by the CourseOffering class.

A good class captures one and only one abstraction—it should have one major theme. For example, a class that has the capability of maintaining information about a student and the information about all the course offerings that the student has taken over the years is not a good class since it does not have one major theme. This class should be split into two related classes: StudentInformation and StudentHistory.

Classes should be named using the vocabulary of the domain. The name should be a singular noun that best characterizes the abstraction. Acronyms may be used if the acronym has the same meaning for all involved, but if an acronym has different meanings for different people, then the full name should always be used. If a class is named with an acronym, the full name should also be contained in the class documentation.

Tool constraints may also affect the naming standards set for a project. In Rational Rose 4.0, an actor is a class that has a stereotype of < <Actor> >. Thus, you cannot have an actor and a class with the same name. I have adopted the convention of appending the word Information to the actor name for all classes that contain information about actors (e.g., StudentInformation). Another option would be to append the word Actor to the actor and then have the class be a simple name (e.g., StudentActor and Student). The bottom line is: Pick a standard for naming classes that conforms to your project and tool and make sure that everyone follows the standard.

It is often hard to distinguish between an object and a class. Why is Algebra 101, Section 1 an object and not a class? What makes it different from Algebra 101, Section 2? The answers to these questions are very subjective. By looking at their structure and behavior, it can be seen that both have the same structure and behavior. They are only different course offerings for a semester. In addition, it may be noted that there are many other things in the Course Registration System that have the same structure and behavior (e.g., Music 101, Section1; History 101, Section 1; and History 101, Section 2). This leads to the decision to create a CourseOffering class.

In the UML, classes are represented as compartmentalized rectangles. The top compartment contains the name of the class, the middle compartment contains the structure of the class (attributes), and the bottom compartment contains the behavior of the class (operations). A class is shown in Figure 4-2.

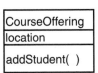

Figure 4-2   UML Notation for a Class

CREATING CLASSES IN THE ROSE BROWSER

1. Right-click to select the Logical View in the browser.
2. Select the New:Class menu choice. A class called New Class is placed in the browser.
3. While the new class is still selected, enter the name of the class.

The browser view of a class is shown in Figure 4-3.

Figure 4-3   Class Created in the Browser

STEREOTYPES AND CLASSES

WE PREVIOUSLY TALKED about stereotypes for relationships in use case diagrams. Classes can also have stereotypes. As before, a stereotype provides the capability to create a new kind of modeling element. Here, we can create new kinds of classes. Some common stereotypes for a class are entity, boundary, control, utility, and exception.

The stereotype for a class is shown below the class name enclosed in guillemets (< < > >). If desired, a graphic icon or a specific color may be associated with a stereotype. For example, all classes with a stereotype of < <exception> > may be drawn in red.

A class with a stereotype of entity is shown in Figure 4-4.

Figure 4-4   Class with a Stereotype

DISCOVERING CLASSES

A COOKBOOK FOR finding classes does not exist. As Grady Booch has been known to say, "This is hard!" The Rational Objectory Process advocates finding the classes for a system under development by looking for boundary, control, and entity classes. These three stereo-types conform to a *model-view-controller* point of view and allow the analyst to partition the system by separating the view from the domain from the control needed by the system.

Since the analysis and design process is iterative, the list of classes will change as time moves on. The initial set of classes probably will not be the set of classes that eventually gets implemented. Thus, the term candidate class is often used to describe the first set of classes found for a system.

Entity Classes

An entity class models information and associated behavior that is generally long lived. This type of class may reflect a real-world entity, or it may be needed to perform tasks internal to the system. They are typically independent of their surroundings; that is, they are not sensitive to how the surroundings communicate with the system. Many times, they are application independent, meaning that they may be used in more than one application.

The first step is to examine the responsibilities documented in the flow of events for the identified use cases (i.e., what the system must do). Entity classes typically are classes that are needed by the system to accomplish some responsibility. The nouns and noun phrases used to describe the responsibility may be a good starting point. The initial list of nouns must be filtered since it could contain nouns that are outside the problem domain, nouns that are just language expressions, nouns that are redundant, and nouns that are descriptions of class structures.

Entity classes typically are found early in the Elaboration Phase. They are often called *domain* classes since they usually deal with abstractions of real-world entities.

Boundary Classes

Boundary classes handle the communication between the system surroundings and the inside of the system. They can provide the interface to a user or another system (i.e., the interface to an actor). They constitute the surroundings-dependent part of the system. Boundary classes are used to model the system interfaces.

Each physical actor/scenario pair is examined to discover boundary classes. The boundary classes chosen in the Elaboration Phase of development are typically at a high level. For example, you may model a window but not model each of its dialogue boxes and buttons. At this point, you are documenting the user interface requirements, not implementing the interface.

User interface requirements tend to be very vague—the terms user-friendly and flexible seem to be used a lot. But user-friendly means different things to different people. This is where proto-typing and storyboarding techniques can be very useful. The customer can get the look and feel of the system and truly capture *what* user-friendly means. The *what* is then captured as the structure and behavior of the boundary class. During design, these classes are refined to take into consideration the chosen user interface mechanisms—how they are to be implemented.

Boundary classes are also added to facilitate communication with other systems. During design, these classes are refined to take into consideration the chosen communication protocols.

Control Classes

Control classes model sequencing behavior specific to one or more use cases. Control classes coordinate the events needed to realize the behavior specified in the use case. You can think of a control class as "running" or "executing" the use case—it represents the dynamics of the use case. Control classes typically are application-dependent classes.

In the early stages of the Elaboration Phase, a control class is added for each actor/use case pair. The control class is responsible for the flow of events in the use case.

The use of control classes is very subjective. Many authors feel that the use of control classes results in behavior being separated from data. This can happen if your control classes are not chosen wisely. If a control class is doing more than sequencing, then it is doing too much! For example, in the course registration system, a student selects a course offering, and if the course offering is available, the student is added to it. Who knows how to add the student—the control class or the course offering? The right answer is the course offering. The control class knows when the student should be added; the course offering knows how to add the student. A bad control class would not only know when to add the student but how to add the student.

The addition of a control class per actor/use case pair is only an initial cut—as analysis and design continues, control classes may be eliminated, split up, or combined.

CREATING STEREOTYPES FOR CLASSES IN RATIONAL ROSE

1. Right-click to select the class in the browser and make the shortcut menu visible.
2. Select the Specification menu choice.
3. Select the General tab.
4. Enter the name of the stereotype.
5. Click the OK button to close the Specification.

The Specification for the StudentInformation class is shown in Figure 4-5.

DOCUMENTING CLASSES

AS CLASSES ARE created, they should also be documented. The documentation should state the purpose of the class and not the structure of the class. For example, a StudentInformation class could be documented as follows:

Figure 4-5   Setting a Class Stereotype

> *Information needed to register and bill students. A student is someone who is registered to take classes at the University.*

A bad definition would be:

> *The name, address, and phone number of a student.*

This definition only tells me the structure of the class, which can be determined by looking at its attributes. It does not tell me why I need the class.

Difficulty in naming or documenting a class may be an indication that it is not a good abstraction. The following list typifies things that can happen as classes are named and documented:

- Can identify a name and a clear concise definition—good candidate class

- Can identify a name, but the definition is the same as another class—combine the classes

- Can identify a name, but need a book to document the purpose—break up the class

- Cannot identify a name or a definition—more analysis is needed to determine the correct abstractions

DOCUMENTING CLASSES IN RATIONAL ROSE

1. Click to select the class in the browser.
2. Position the cursor in the documentation window and enter the documentation for the class.

The description of the StudentInformation class is shown in Figure 4-6.

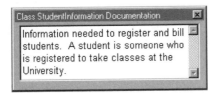

Figure 4-6   Class Documentation

PACKAGES

IF A SYSTEM contained only a few classes, you could manage them easily. Most systems are composed of many classes, and thus you need a mechanism to group them together for ease of use, maintainability, and reusability. This is where the concept of a package is useful. A package in the logical view of the model is a collection of related packages and/or classes. By grouping classes into packages, we can look at the higher level view of the model (i.e., the packages), or we can dig deeper into the model by looking at what is contained by the package.

Each package contains an interface that is realized by its set of public classes—those classes to which classes in other packages talk. The rest of the classes in a package are implementation classes—classes, do not communicate with classes in other packages.

If the system is complex, packages may be created early in the Elaboration Phase to facilitate communication. For simpler systems, the classes found early in analysis may be grouped into one package—the system itself. As analysis and design progress, the concept of a package will be used to group the classes that are needed to carry out the architectural decisions made for the system.

In the UML, packages are represented as folders. A package is shown in Figure 4-7.

Figure 4-7   UML Notation for a Package

CREATING PACKAGES IN THE ROSE BROWSER

1. Right-click to select the Logical View in the browser.
2. Select the New:Package menu choice.
3. While the package is still selected, enter the name of the package.

A package created via the browser is shown in Figure 4-8. As packages are created, classes in the model are relocated.

RELOCATING CLASSES IN THE ROSE BROWSER

1. Click to select the class in the browser.
2. Drag the class to the desired package.
3. Repeat the steps for each class that is to be relocated.

Figure 4-8   Package Created in the Browser

Relocated classes are shown in Figure 4-9.

Figure 4-9   Relocated Classes

OBJECTS AND CLASSES IN THE ESU COURSE REGISTRATION PROBLEM

WE WILL LOOK at the *Add a Course Offering to Teach* scenario, which is one of the subflows of the *Select Courses to Teach* use case. The main capability provided by this scenario is the ability of the professor to select a course offering to teach for a given semester.

Although we are looking at this process in a step-by-step manner, many of these steps may occur concurrently in the real world.

Identify Boundary Classes

This use case interacts only with the Professor actor. The action specified in this scenario is only one capability provided by the use case (the use case also states that the Professor can modify a selection, delete a selection, review a selection, and print a selection). This means that something in the system must provide the capability for the Professor to select a capability. A class containing all the options available to the Professor as stated in the use case is created to satisfy this need. This class is called ProfessorCourseOptions. Additionally, we can identify a class that deals with the addition of a new Course Offering for the Professor. This class is called AddACourseOffering.

Identify Entity Classes

This scenario deals with courses, their course offerings, and the professor assignment. We can identify three entity classes: Course, CourseOffering, and ProfessorInformation.

Identify Control Classes

We will add one control class to handle the flow of events for the use case. This class is called ProfessorCourseManager.

The identified classes have been added to the model as shown in Figure 4-10.

Figure 4-10   Classes for the **Add a Course Offering to Teach** *Scenario*

Create Packages

The next step is to group classes into packages. At this time, we have identified six classes: Course, CourseOffering, ProfessorInformation, ProfessorCourseOptions, AddACourseOffering, and Professor-CourseManager. They fall into three logical groups—things unique to the University, things that contain information about people, and things that are interfaces to actors. We can identify packages: Interfaces, UniversityArtifacts, and People. The classes are relocated to the identified packages. The packages along with their contained classes are shown in Figure 4-11.

Figure 4-11   Packages in the Browser

CLASS DIAGRAMS

AS MORE AND more classes are added to the model, a textual representation of the classes is not sufficient. Class diagrams are created to provide a picture or view of some or all of the classes in the model.

The Main class diagram in the logical view of the model is typically a picture of the packages in the system. Each package also has its own Main class diagram, which typically displays the public classes of the package. Other diagrams are created as needed. Some typical uses of other diagrams are:

- View of all the implementation classes in a package
- View of the structure and behavior of one or more class
- View of an inheritance hierarchy

THE MAIN CLASS DIAGRAM IN RATIONAL ROSE

Rose automatically creates the Main class diagram in the Logical View of the model.

To add packages to the Main class diagram:

1. Double-click on the Main diagram in the browser to open the diagram.
2. Click to select the package in the browser.
3. Drag the package onto the diagram.
4. Repeat the preceding steps for each package that is to be added to the diagram.

The Main class diagram for the Registration System is shown in Figure 4-12.

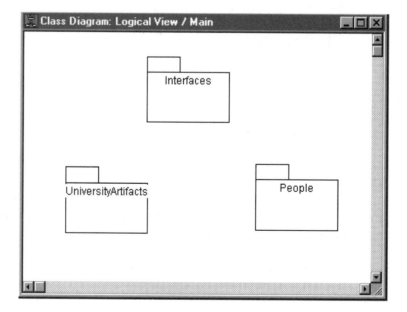

Figure 4-12   Main Class Diagram

CREATING A PACKAGE MAIN CLASS DIAGRAM IN RATIONAL ROSE

1. Double-click on the package on a class diagram.
2. Rose will open the package and create (or display) the Main class diagram for the package.
3. Click to select a class in the browser and drag the class onto the diagram.
4. Repeat step 3 for each additional class that is to be placed on the diagram.

The Main class diagram for the UniversityArtifacts package is shown in Figure 4-13. Notice that the CourseOffering class is not on the diagram. This is an implementation class in the package and we decided not to show it on the Main diagram of the package.

Figure 4-13   UniversityArtifacts Package Main Class Diagram

As more packages and classes are added to the model, additional diagrams are created as needed.

Class diagrams may also be created in the use case view of the model. These diagrams typically are attached to use cases and contain a view of the classes participating in the use case.

CREATING A VIEW OF PARTICIPATING CLASSES IN RATIONAL ROSE

1. Right-click on the use case in the browser to make the shortcut menu visible.
2. Select the New:Class Diagram menu choice.
3. While the diagram is still selected, enter the name of the class diagram.
4. Double-click on the diagram in the browser to open the diagram.
5. Click to select a class in the logical view of the browser and drag the class onto the diagram.
6. Repeat step 5 for each additional class that is to be placed onto the diagram.

The View of Participating Classes for the *Select Courses to Teach* use case is shown in Figure 4-14.

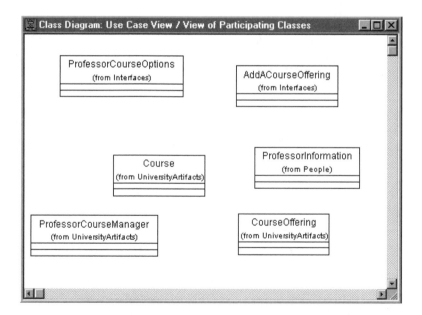

Figure 4-14   View of Participating Classes

You will notice that the visibility (package owning the class) of the class is shown in Figure 4-14.

TO SET VISIBILITY DISPLAY IN RATIONAL ROSE

To set the default visibility display:

1. Select the Tools:Options menu choice.
2. Select the Diagram tab.
3. Select the Show Visibility checkbox to set the default to show the visibility of all classes.

To set the visibility for a selected class:

1. Right-click to select the class on a diagram and make the shortcut menu visible.
2. Click to select or deselect the Show Visibility menu choice.

Stereotypes may also be shown on a class diagram.

TO SHOW THE STEREOTYPE IN RATIONAL ROSE

1. Right-click on the class in a class diagram to make the shortcut menu visible.
2. Select the Show Stereotype menu choice.

A class diagram displaying stereotype names is shown in Figure 4-15.

SUMMARY

AN OBJECT IS a computer representation of an entity, either real-world or invented. An object is a concept, abstraction, or thing with sharp boundaries and meaning for an application. Each object in a system has three characteristics: state, behavior, and identity. The state of an object is one of the possible conditions in which it may exist. Behavior determines how an object acts and reacts to requests from other objects. Identity states that each object is unique—even if its state is identical to that of another object.

A class is a description of a group of objects with common properties (attributes), common behavior (operations), common relationships to other objects (associations and aggregations), and common

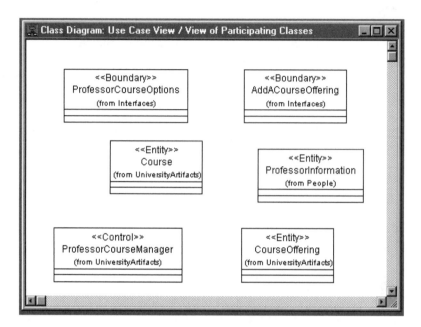

Figure 4-15   Class Diagram with Stereotype Display

semantics. In the UML, a class is drawn as a compartmentalized rectangle. The compartments show the class name, its structure, and its
behavior. As classes are created, they should also be documented.
The documentation should state the purpose of the class and not
the structure of the class.

Stereotypes provide the capability to create a new type of
modeling element. Stereotypes must be based on elements that
are part of the UML metamodel. During analysis, three common
stereotypes for a class are entity, boundary, and control. These
stereotypes are useful in defining the classes needed for a system
under development.

A package in the logical view of the model is a collection of
related packages and/or classes. By grouping classes into packages,
we can look at the higher level view of the model (i.e., the packages), or we can dig deeper into the model by looking at what is
contained by the package.

Class diagrams are created to provide a picture or view of some or all of the classes in the model. Class diagrams may also be created in the use case view of the model. These diagrams typically are attached to use cases and contain a view of the classes participating in the use case.

Chapter 5

Discovering
Object Interaction

USE CASE REALIZATION

THE USE CASE diagram presents an outside view of the system. The functionality of the use case is captured in the flow of events. Scenarios are used to describe how use cases are realized as interactions among societies of objects. A scenario is an instance of a use case—it is one path through the flow of events for the use case. Scenarios are developed to help identify the objects, the classes, and the object interactions needed to carry out a piece of the functionality specified by the use case. Scenarios document decisions about how the responsibilities specified in the use cases are distributed among the objects and classes in the system. They also provide an excellent communication medium to be used in the discussion of the system requirements with customers. "Scenarios speak the language of the end user and the domain expert, and therefore provide a means for them to state their expectations about the desired behavior of a system to its developers."[1]

Each use case is a web of scenarios—primary scenarios (the normal flow for the use case) and secondary scenarios (the what-if logic of the use case). This means that there are numerous scenarios for any given system—all the primary and secondary scenarios for all the use cases. During the early stage of analysis it is safe to say that looking at the primary scenarios for each identified use case is enough. When you find that each new scenario is repeating a lot of steps from previously identified scenarios, then you have reached the finish line. "This phase of analysis should be drawn to a close once the team has elaborated approximately 80% of a system's primary scenarios along with a representative selection of the secondary ones. Elaborate upon any more, and your analysis will likely reach diminishing returns; elaborate upon any fewer, and you won't have a sufficient understanding of the desired behavior of the system to properly understand the risks."[2]

---

[1] Booch, Grady. *Object Solutions,* Redwood City, CA: Addison-Wesley, 1995.

[2] *Ibid.*

DOCUMENTING SCENARIOS

THE FLOW OF events for a use case is captured in text, whereas scenarios are captured in interaction diagrams. There are two types of interaction diagrams—sequence diagrams and collaboration diagrams. Each diagram is a graphical view of the scenario.

SEQUENCE DIAGRAMS

A SEQUENCE DIAGRAM shows object interactions arranged in time sequence. It depicts the objects and classes involved in the scenario and the sequence of messages exchanged between the objects needed to carry out the functionality of the scenario. Sequence diagrams typically are associated with use cases in the model of the system under development.

In the UML, an object in a sequence diagram is drawn as a rectangle containing the name of the object, underlined. An object can be named in one of three ways: the object name, the object name and its class, or just the class name (anonymous object). The three ways of naming an object are shown in Figure 5-1.

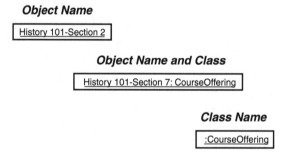

Figure 5-1   Naming Objects in a Sequence Diagram

Object names can be specific (e.g., Algebra 101, Section 1), or they can be general (e.g., a course offering). Often, an anonymous object (class name only) may be used to represent any object in the class.

Each object also has its timeline represented by a dashed line below the object. Messages between objects are represented by arrows that point from the client (sender of the message) to the supplier (receiver of the message).

The UML notation for objects and messages in a sequence diagram is shown in Figure 5-2.

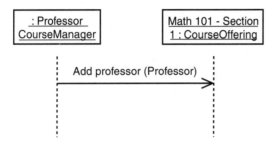

Figure 5-2   UML Notation for Objects and Messages in a Sequence Diagram

CREATING A SEQUENCE DIAGRAM IN RATIONAL ROSE

1. Right-click to select the use case in the browser and make the shortcut menu visible.
2. Select the New:Sequence Diagram menu choice. An unnamed sequence diagram is added to the browser.
3. With the new sequence diagram selected, enter the name of the sequence diagram.

The browser view of a sequence diagram is shown in Figure 5-3.

Figure 5-3   Browser View of a Sequence Diagram

CREATING OBJECTS AND MESSAGES IN SEQUENCE DIAGRAMS IN RATIONAL ROSE

1. Double-click on the sequence diagram in the browser to open the diagram.
2. Click to select the actor in the browser.
3. Drag the actor onto the sequence diagram.
4. Click to select the object icon from the toolbar.
5. Click on the sequence diagram window to place the object.
6. While the object is still selected, enter the name of the object.
7. Repeat the preceding steps for each object and actor in the scenario.
8. Click to select the object message icon from the toolbar.
9. Click on the actor or object sending the message and drag the message line to the actor or object receiving the message.
10. While the message line is still selected, enter the name of the message.
11. Repeat steps 7 through 9 for each message in the scenario.

The sequence diagram for the *Create a Course* scenario is shown in Figure 5-4.

Figure 5-4   Sequence Diagram

**ASSIGNING OBJECTS IN A SEQUENCE
DIAGRAM TO CLASSES IN RATIONAL ROSE**

1. Click to select the class in the browser.
2. Drag the class onto the object in the sequence diagram. Rose will add the class name preceded by a: to the object name. If the object is unnamed, the name is set to :class-Name.

A sequence diagram with objects assigned to classes is shown in Figure 5-5.

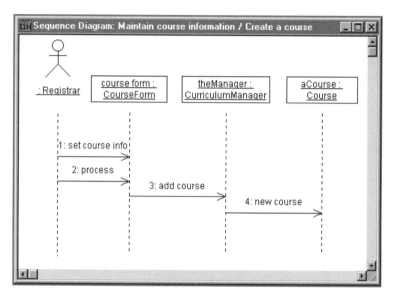

Figure 5-5   Sequence Diagram with Objects Assigned to Classes

SEQUENCE DIAGRAMS AND BOUNDARY CLASSES

BOUNDARY CLASSES ARE added to sequence diagrams to show the interaction with the user or another system. In the early analysis phases, the purpose of showing boundary classes on a sequence diagram is to capture and document the interface requirements, NOT to show how the interface will be implemented. The actual messages from the actor to the boundary class along with their sequencing information are dependent upon the application framework that is chosen later in development; thus, they will probably change as more of the "how" is added to the system.

COMPLEXITY AND SEQUENCE DIAGRAMS

EVERY TIME I teach a class, the question "How complex can a sequence diagram be?" is always asked. The answer I always give is, "Keep it simple." The beauty of these diagrams is their simplicity—it is very easy to see the objects, the object interactions, the messages between the objects, and the functionality captured by the scenario.

The next question is usually "What do I do about conditional logic?" (all the *if, then, else* logic that exists in the real world). Here, you again have a very subjective answer. If the logic is simple, involving only a few messages, I usually add the logic to one diagram and use notes and scripts to communicate the choices to be made. On the other hand, if the *if, then, else* logic involves many complicated messages, I typically draw a separate diagram—one for the *if* case, one for the *then* case, and one for the *else* case. This is done to keep the diagrams simple.

COLLABORATION DIAGRAMS

A COLLABORATION DIAGRAM is an alternate way to show a scenario. This type of diagram shows object interactions organized around the objects and their links to each other. A collaboration diagram contains:

- Objects drawn as rectangles
- Links between objects shown as lines connecting the linked objects
- Messages shown as text and an arrow that points from the client to the supplier

The UML notation for objects, links, and messages in a collaboration diagram is shown in Figure 5-6.

CREATING COLLABORATION DIAGRAMS FROM SEQUENCE DIAGRAMS IN RATIONAL ROSE

1. Double-click on the sequence diagram in the browser to open the diagram.
2. Choose the Browse:Create Collaboration Diagram menu choice or press the F5 key.
3. Rearrange the objects and messages on the diagram as needed.

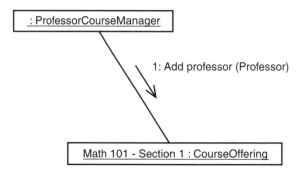

Figure 5-6   UML Notation for Objects, Links, and Messages in a Collaboration Diagram

The collaboration diagram is shown in Figure 5-7.

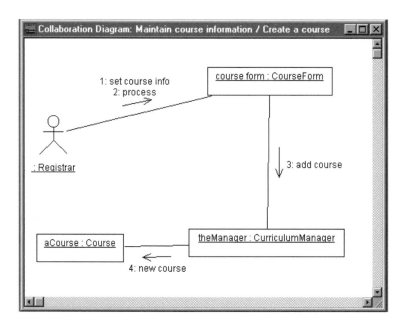

Figure 5-7   Collaboration Diagram

Collaboration diagrams can also be created from scratch. In that case, a sequence diagram can be created from the collaboration diagram by selecting the Browse:Create Sequence Diagram menu choice or pressing the F5 key.

WHY ARE THERE TWO DIFFERENT DIAGRAMS?

SEQUENCE DIAGRAMS PROVIDE a way to look at a scenario in a time-based order—what happens first, what happens next. Customers easily can read and understand this type of diagram. Hence, they are very useful in the early analysis phases. Collaboration diagrams tend to provide the big picture for a scenario since the collaborations are organized around the object links to one another. These diagrams seem to be used more in the design phase of development when you are designing the implementation of the relationships.

SEQUENCE DIAGRAM FOR THE ESU COURSE REGISTRATION SYSTEM

CONTINUING WITH OUR analysis of the *Add a Course Offering* scenario, the diagram is shown in Figure 5-8.

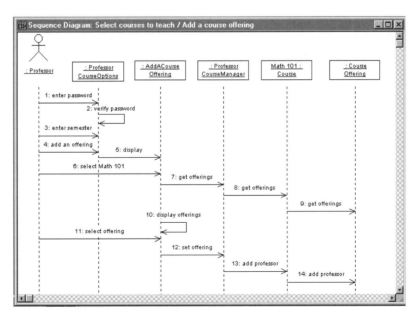

Figure 5-8   Sequence Diagram for the **Add a Course Offering** *Scenario*

SUMMARY

THE USE CASE diagram presents an outside view of the system. The functionality of the use case is captured in the flow of events. Scenarios are used to describe how use cases are realized as interactions among societies of objects. A scenario is an instance of a use case—it is one path through the flow of events for the use case. Thus, each use case is a web of scenarios. Scenarios are developed to help identify the objects, the classes, and the object interactions needed to carry out a piece of the functionality specified by the use case.

The flow of events for use cases are typically captured in text, whereas scenarios are captured in interaction diagrams. There are two types of interaction diagrams—sequence diagrams and collaboration diagrams. Each diagram is a graphical view of the scenario.

A sequence diagram shows object interactions arranged in time sequence. A collaboration diagram is an alternate way to show a scenario. This type of diagram shows object interactions organized around the objects and their links to each other.

Chapter 6

Specifying Relationships

THE NEED FOR RELATIONSHIPS

ALL SYSTEMS ARE made up of many classes and objects. System behavior is achieved through the collaboration of the objects in the system. For example, a student is added to a course offering when the course offering receives the *add student* message. This is often referred to as an object sending a message to another object. Relationships provide the conduit for object interaction. Two types of relationships discovered during analysis are *associations* and *aggregations.*

ASSOCIATION RELATIONSHIPS

AN ASSOCIATION IS a bidirectional semantic connection between classes. It is not a data flow as defined in structured analysis and design—data may flow in either direction across the association. An association between classes means that there is a link between objects in the associated classes. For example, an association between the Course class and the StudentInformation class means that objects in the Course class are connected to objects in the StudentInformation class. The number of objects connected depends upon the multiplicity of the association, which is discussed later in this chapter. In the UML, association relationships are shown as lines connecting the associated classes, as shown in Figure 6-1.

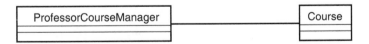

Figure 6-1   UML Notation for an Association Relationship

 CREATING AN ASSOCIATION RELATIONSHIP IN RATIONAL ROSE
1. Click to select the association icon from the toolbar.
2. Click on one of the associated classes in a class diagram.
3. Drag the association line to the other associated class.

An association relationship is shown in Figure 6-2.

Figure 6-2   Association Relationship

AGGREGATION RELATIONSHIPS

AN AGGREGATION RELATIONSHIP is a specialized form of association in which a whole is related to its part(s). Aggregation is known as a "part-of" or containment relationship. The UML notation for an aggregation relationship is an association with a diamond next to the class denoting the aggregate (whole), as shown in Figure 6-3.

Figure 6-3   UML Notation for an Aggregation Relationship

The following tests may be used to determine if an association should be an aggregation:

- Is the phrase "part of" used to describe the relationship?
- Are some operations on the whole automatically applied to its parts? For example, delete a course, then delete all of its course offerings.
- Is there an intrinsic asymmetry to the relationship where one class is subordinate to the other?

For example, a Course (Math 101) may be offered at different times during a semester. Each offering is represented as a Course Offering (e.g., Math 101, Section 1 and Math 101, Section 2). The relationship between a Course and a CourseOffering is modeled as an aggregation—a Course "has" CourseOfferings.

CREATING AN AGGREGATION RELATIONSHIP IN RATIONAL ROSE

1. Select the aggregation icon from the toolbar.
2. Click on the class playing the role of the "part" in a class diagram and drag the aggregation line to the class playing the role of the "whole."

An aggregation relationship is shown in Figure 6-4.

ASSOCIATION OR AGGREGATION?

IF TWO CLASSES are tightly bound by a whole-part relationship, the relationship is typically an aggregation. "The decision to use aggregation is a matter of judgment and is often arbitrary. Often it is not obvious if an association should be modeled as an aggregation. If you exercise careful judgment and are consistent, the imprecise distinction between aggregation and ordinary association does not cause problems in practice."[1]

---

[1] Rumbaugh, James, et al. *Object-Oriented Modeling and Design.* Prentice Hall, Englewood Cliffs, NJ, 1991. Page 58.

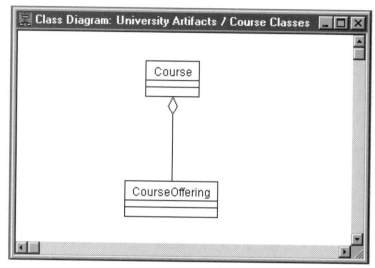

Figure 6-4   Aggregation Relationship

Whether a relationship is an association or an aggregation is often domain dependent. What type of relationship should be used to model a car with its tires? If the application is a service center, and the only reason you care about the tire is because it is part of the car you are servicing, then the relationship should be an aggregation. On the other hand, if the application is a tire store, you will care about the tire independent of the car, and therefore the relationship should be an association.

NAMING RELATIONSHIPS

AN ASSOCIATION MAY be named. Usually the name is an active verb or verb phrase that communicates the meaning of the relationship. Since the verb phase typically implies a reading direction, it is desirable to name the association so it reads correctly from left to right or top to bottom. The words may have to be changed to read the association in the other direction (e.g., a Professor *teaches* a Course, a Course *is taught by* a Professor). It is important to note that the name of the association is optional. Names are added if they are needed to add clarity to the model. Aggregation relationships typically are not named since they are read using the words "has" or "contains."

NAMING RELATIONSHIPS IN RATIONAL ROSE

1. Click to select the relationship line on a class diagram.
2. Enter the name of the relationship.

A named relationship is shown in Figure 6-5.

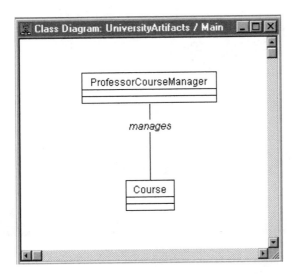

Figure 6-5   A Named Association

ROLE NAMES

THE END OF an association where it connects to a class is called an association role. Role names can be used instead of association names. A role name is a noun that denotes the purpose or capacity wherein one class associates with another. The role name is placed on the association near the class that it modifies. A role name may be placed on one or both ends of an association line. It is not necessary to have both a role name and an association name.

CREATING ROLE NAMES IN RATIONAL ROSE

1. Right-click on the relationship line near the class that it
    modifies to make the shortcut menu visible.
2. Select the Role Name menu choice.
3. Enter the name of the role.

Figure 6-6 shows an association with a role name.

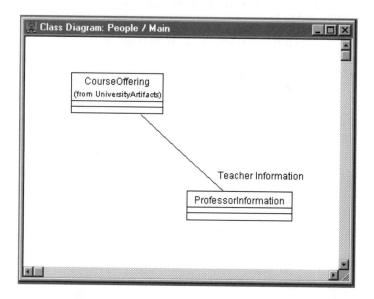

Figure 6-6   Role Name

The relationship shown in Figure 6-6 is read in both directions.

- ProfessorInformation playing the role of the Teacher
  Information is related to the CourseOffering

- CourseOffering is related to ProfessorInformation
  playing the role of Teacher Information

There is no standard as to whether you should use association
names or role names. However, most people today tend to use role
names instead of association names since it is easier to convey the
meaning of the relationship. This is especially true in a bidirectional
relationship since it is very hard to find a verb phase that reads cor-

rectly in both directions. What verb phrase could be used to name the association in Figure 6-6? By using a role name, the meaning is clear in both directions.

Associations are named or role names are used only when the names are needed for clarity. If you have a relationship between Company and Person, then you could use an association name called "employs" or the role names of "Employer" and "Employee" to convey an employment relationship. If the classes were named Employer and Employee, no name would be necessary since the meaning of the relationship is clear based on the names of the classes.

MULTIPLICITY INDICATORS

ALTHOUGH MULTIPLICITY IS specified for classes, it defines the number of objects that participate in a relationship. Multiplicity defines the number of objects that are linked to one another. There are two multiplicity indicators for each association or aggregation—one at each end of the line. Some common multiplicity indicators are:

1	Exactly one
0..*	Zero or more
1..*	One or more
0..1	Zero or one
5..8	Specific range (5, 6, 7, or 8)
4..7,9	Combination (4, 5, 6, 7, or 9)

CREATING MULTIPLICITY IN RATIONAL ROSE

1. Double-click on the relationship line to make the Specification visible.
2. Select the Detail tab for the role being modified (Role A Detail or Role B Detail).
3. Enter the desired multiplicity.

Multiplicity indicators are shown in Figure 6-7.

Figure 6-7   Multiplicity Indicators

The drawing in Figure 6-7 may be read using the following words:

- One CourseOffering object is related to *exactly one* ProfessorInformation object playing the role of the Teacher Information. For example, Math 101, Section 1 (a CourseOffering object) is related to Professor Smith (a ProfessorInformation object).

- One ProfessorInformation object playing the role of the Teacher Information is related to *zero to four* CourseOffering objects. For example, Professor Smith (a ProfessorInformation object) is related to Math 101, Section 1; Algebra 200, Section 2; and Calculus 1, Section 3 (CourseOffering objects). Since the multiplicity is a range of zero to four, as few as zero CourseOffering objects to a maximum of four CourseOffering objects may be linked to one ProfessorInformation object.

REFLEXIVE RELATIONSHIPS

MULTIPLE OBJECTS BELONGING to the same class may have to communicate with one another. This is shown on the class diagram as a reflexive association or aggregation. Role names rather than association names typically are used for reflexive relationships.

CREATING A REFLEXIVE RELATIONSHIP IN RATIONAL ROSE

1. Select the association (or aggregation) icon from the toolbar.
2. Click on the class and drag the association (or aggregation) line outside the class.
3. Release the mouse button.
4. Click and drag the association (or aggregation) line back to the class.
5. Enter the role names and multiplicity for each end of the reflexive association (or aggregation).

A reflexive relationship is shown in Figure 6-8.

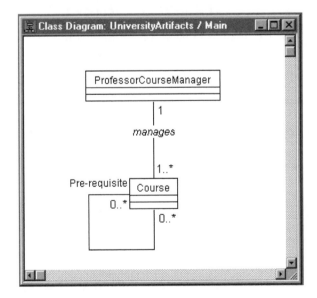

Figure 6-8   Reflexive Relationship

The reflexive relationship in Figure 6-8 may be read using the following words:

- One Course object playing the role of Prerequisite is related to zero or more Course objects

- One Course object is related to zero or more Course objects playing the role of Prerequisite

FINDING RELATIONSHIPS

SCENARIOS ARE EXAMINED to determine if a relationship should exist between two classes. Messages between objects mean that the objects must communicate with each other. Associations and/or aggregations provide the pathway for communication.

Relationships may also be discovered based on the signature of an operation. This is discussed in Chapter 7.

RELATIONSHIPS IN THE ESU COURSE REGISTRATION PROBLEM

IN THE *ADD a Course Offering* scenario, the communicating objects along with the relationship type decisions that have been made are shown in Table 6-1.

Sending Class	Receiving Class	Relationship Type
ProfessorCourseOptions	AddACourseOffering	Aggregation
AddACourseOffering	ProfessorCourseManager	Association
ProfessorCourseManager	Course	Association
Course	CourseOffering	Aggregation

Table 6-1   Class Relationships

A class diagram with the added relationships is shown in Figure 6-9.

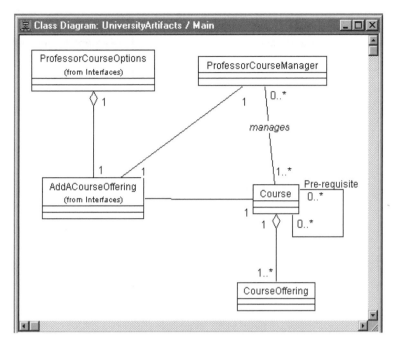

Figure 6-9   Relationships in the **Add a Course Offering** *Scenario*

PACKAGE RELATIONSHIPS

PACKAGE RELATIONSHIPS ARE also added to the model. The type of relationship is a dependency relationship, shown as a dashed arrow to the dependent package, as shown in Figure 6-10. If package A is dependent on package B, this implies that one or more classes in package A initiates communication with one or more public classes in package B. Package A is referred to as the Client package, and package B is referred to as the Supplier package. Package relationships are also discovered by examining the scenarios and class relationships for the system under development. As this is an iterative process, the relationships will change as analysis and design progress.

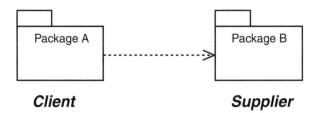

Figure 6-10   Package Relationships

PACKAGE RELATIONSHIPS IN THE COURSE REGISTRATION PROBLEM

IN THE *ADD a Course Offering* scenario, the AddACourseOffering class sends a message to the ProfessorCourseManager class. This implies that there is a relationship between the Interfaces package and the UniversityArtifacts package. At this time, we have not discovered any relationships to the People package.

CREATING PACKAGE RELATIONSHIPS IN RATIONAL ROSE

1. Select the dependency relationship icon from the toolbar.
2. Click on the dependent package and drag the arrow to the package it depends upon.

The package relationships for the Course Registration System are shown in Figure 6-11.

SUMMARY

RELATIONSHIPS PROVIDE THE conduit for object interaction. Two types of relationships between classes that are discovered during analysis are associations and aggregations. An association is a bidirectional semantic connection between classes. An aggregation is a specialized form of association in which a whole is related to its part(s).

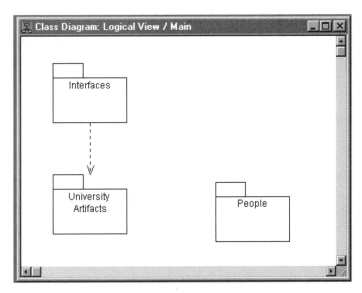

Figure 6-11   Package Relationships in the ESU Course Registration System

An association may be named. Usually the name is an active verb or verb phrase that communicates the meaning of the relationship. Roles can be used instead of association names. A role name is a noun that denotes the purpose or capacity wherein one class associates with another. Multiplicity is the number of instances that participate in a relationship. There are two multiplicity indicators for each association or aggregation—one at each end of the relationship line.

Multiple objects belonging to the same class may have to communicate with one another. This is shown on the class diagram as a reflexive association or aggregation.

Scenarios are examined to determine if a relationship should exist between two classes.

Packages are related via dependency relationships. If package A is dependent on package B, this implies that one or more classes in package A initiates communication with one or more public classes in package B.

Chapter 7

Adding Behavior and Structure

REPRESENTING BEHAVIOR AND STRUCTURE

A CLASS EMBODIES a set of responsibilities that define the behavior of the objects in the class. The responsibilities are carried out by the operations defined for the class. An operation should do only one thing, and it should do it well! For example, a CourseOffering class needs to be able to add a student and remove a student. These responsibilities are represented by two operations—one that knows how to add a student, and one that knows how to remove a student. All instances of the class will be able to perform the identified operations of the class.

The structure of an object is described by the attributes of the class. Each attribute is a data definition held by objects of the class. Objects defined for the class have a value for every attribute of the class. For example, a Course class has the attributes of name, definition, and number of credit hours. This implies that every Course object will have a value for each attribute. Attribute values do not have to be unique—there are many three-credit courses in the university.

As with classes, style guides should be followed while defining attributes and operations to provide for more readable and maintainable code. In this case study, attributes and operations start with a lowercase letter and underscores are not used—names composed of multiple words are pushed together and the first letter of each additional word is capitalized (e.g., numberOfStudents). Care should be taken to ensure that appropriate style guides are followed for all defined attributes and operations. This provides consistency across the classes, which leads to more maintainable models and code.

If an object in a class does not need an attribute or operation, look at the class definition. This may be a sign that the class is not cohesive and should be broken up into separate classes. For example, suppose the CourseOffering class had the following attributes: offerNumber, location, timeOfDay, department, numberOfferingsInDepartment. A CourseOffering may care about its department, but it probably does not care about the number of other offerings in the department. A better model would be a CourseOffering class related to a Department class. This is in keeping with the general rule that a class should have a major theme.

CREATING OPERATIONS

MESSAGES IN INTERACTION diagrams typically are mapped to operations of the receiving class. However, there are some special cases where the message does not become an operation. If the receiving class is a boundary class that is a placeholder for a graphical user interface (GUI) type class, the message is a statement of the requirements for the GUI. These types of messages typically are implemented as some type of GUI control (i.e., a button) and are not mapped to operations since the behavior is carried out by the control itself. For example, the Professor actor must enter a password to start the *Add a CourseOffering* scenario. This is represented as a message to the boundary class ProfessorCourseOptions. This will never be an operation of the user interface class—it will most likely be a text field on a window. Messages to and from actors also receive special consideration. If the message is to or from an actor that represents a physical person, the message is a statement of human procedure and is therefore incorporated into a user manual, but not to an operation, since it does not make sense to create operations for humans. In the *Add a CourseOffering* scenario, the fact that the professor must have some sort of password to activate the system is an important requirement that should be captured in the user manual. If the message is to or from an actor that represents an external system, a class is created to hold the protocol that is used to perform the communication with the external system. In this case, the message is mapped to an operation of the class.

Operations should be named in terms of the class performing the operation, not the class asking for the functionality to be performed. For example, the operation to add a student to a course offering is called *addStudent()*. Additionally, operation names should not reflect the implementation of the operation since the implementation may change over time. For example, each CourseOffering object has a maximum of ten students assigned to it. You may need to ask the CourseOffering object how many students are assigned to it at a point in time. Today, the number is calculated by looking at the links from the CourseOffering object to StudentInformation objects. An operation called calculateNumberOfStudents() implies there is a calculation involved. Although this is the case today, it may not always be true (next year, the implementation may change to store the value in a file).

MAPPING MESSAGES TO NEW OPERATIONS IN RATIONAL ROSE

1. Assign the objects to classes if that has not been done previously.
2. Right-click on the message arrow to make the shortcut menu visible.
3. Select the < new operation > menu choice. This will open the Operation Specification.
4. Enter the name of the operation in the Operation Specification.
5. Click the OK button to close the Operation Specification.
6. Right-click on the message arrow to make the shortcut menu visible.
7. Select the operation from the list of operations for the class.

Note: If the desired operation already exists for the class, you do not have to re-create the operation; simply select the operation from the list of operations for the class.

A sequence diagram with operations is shown in Figure 7-1.

Operations may also be created independently of interaction diagrams, since not all scenarios are represented in a diagram. This is also true for operations that are created to help another operation. For example, a course might have to determine if a specified professor is certified to teach it before it adds the professor as the teacher. An operation called validateProfessor() could be an operation created to perform this behavior.

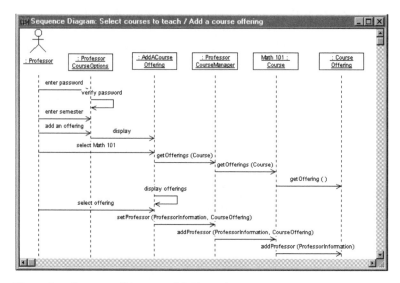

Figure 7-1   Sequence Diagram with Operations

CREATING OPERATIONS IN RATIONAL ROSE

1. Right-click to select the class in the browser and make the pop-up menu visible.
2. Select the New:Operation menu choice. This will create an operation called opname in the browser.
3. With the new operation selected, enter the desired name.

Operations for the Course class are shown in Figure 7-2.

DOCUMENTING OPERATIONS

EACH OPERATION SHOULD be documented so the reader of the model can quickly understand its purpose. The documentation should state the functionality performed by the operation. It should also state any input values needed by the operation along with the return value of the operation. The input and return values constitute the operation signature. This information may not be known initially. Instead, it may be added later in the life cycle when more is known about the class.

Figure 7-2   Operations in the Browser

DOCUMENTING OPERATIONS IN RATIONAL ROSE

1. Click the + next to the class in the browser to expand the class.
2. Click to select the operation.
3. Position the cursor in the documentation window and enter the documentation for the operation.

The documentation for the addProfessor() operation of the Course class is shown in Figure 7-3.

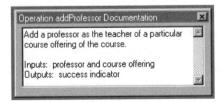

Figure 7-3   Operation Documentation

RELATIONSHIPS
AND OPERATION SIGNATURES

THE SIGNATURE OF an operation may indicate a relationship. If the class for an argument of an operation or the return from an operation is a fundamental class such as a String, the relationship typically is not shown on a diagram. For other classes (i.e., nonfundamental classes), the relationship is typically displayed on one or more class diagrams. For example, the two inputs to the addProfessor() operation of the Course class are professor (ProfessorInformation class) and course offering (CourseOffering class). This implies that relationships exist between:

- Course and ProfessorInformation
- Course and CourseOffering

Relationships based on operation signatures initially are modeled as associations that may be refined into dependency relationships as the design of the system matures. Refinement is covered in Chapter 12. Package relationships should also be reviewed as relationships based on operation signatures are added to the model. For example, we have now added a relationship between the Course class and the ProfessorInformation class. This implies that there is a dependency relationship between the University Artifacts package and the People package.

CREATING ATTRIBUTES

MANY OF THE attributes of a class are found in the problem statement, the set of system requirements, and the flow of events documentation. They may also be discovered when supplying the definition of a class. Finally, domain expertise is also a good source of attributes for a class. For example, the requirements state that information such as course name, description, and number of credit hours is available in the course catalog for a semester. This implies that name, description, and number of credit hours are attributes of the Course class.

CREATING ATTRIBUTES IN RATIONAL ROSE

1. Right-click to select the class in the browser and make the pop-up menu visible.
2. Select the New:Attribute menu choice. This will create an attribute called Name in the browser.
3. With the new attribute selected, enter the desired name.

Attributes for the Course class are shown in Figure 7-4.

Figure 7-4   Attributes in the Browser

DOCUMENTING ATTRIBUTES

ATTRIBUTES SHOULD ALSO be documented with a clear, concise definition. The definition should state the purpose of the attribute, not the structure of the attribute. For example, a bad definition for the name attribute of the Course class could be "a character string of length 15." A better definition for the name attribute is "the title of the course that is used in all University publications."

DOCUMENTING ATTRIBUTES IN RATIONAL ROSE

1. Click the + next to the class in the browser to expand the class.
2. Click to select the attribute.
3. Position the cursor in the documentation window and enter the documentation for the attribute.

The documentation for the name attribute of the Course class is shown in Figure 7-5.

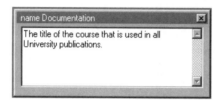

Figure 7-5   Attribute Documentation

DISPLAYING ATTRIBUTES AND OPERATIONS

ATTRIBUTES AND OPERATIONS may be displayed on a class diagram. Often, a class diagram is created specifically for this purpose—it shows the structure and behavior of the classes in a package. Relationships typically are not shown on this diagram.

CREATING A CLASS DIAGRAM TO SHOW THE
ATTRIBUTES AND OPERATIONS FOR A PACKAGE

1. Right-click to select the package in the browser and make the shortcut menu visible.
2. Select the New:Class Diagram menu choice. A class diagram called NewDiagram will be added to the browser.
3. With the new diagram selected, enter the name of the diagram.

ADDING CLASSES TO A DIAGRAM USING THE QUERY MENU

1. Double-click on the diagram in the browser to open the diagram.
2. Select the Query:Add Classes menu choice.
3. Select the desired package.
4. Click to select the desired classes and click the > > > button to add the classes to the diagram or click the All > > button to add all the classes to the diagram.

FILTERING RELATIONSHIPS IN RATIONAL ROSE

1. Double-click on the diagram in the browser to open the diagram.
2. Select the Query:Filter Relationships menu choice.
3. Click the None button in the Type field to hide all relationships shown on the open diagram.
4. Click the OK button to close the Relations window.

DISPLAYING SOME ATTRIBUTES OR OPERATIONS IN RATIONAL ROSE

1. Right-click to select the class on an open class diagram and make the shortcut menu visible.
2. Select the Edit Compartment menu choice.
3. Click to select the attributes and operations to be displayed.
4. Click the > > > button.
5. Click the OK button to close the Edit Compartment window.

SHOWING ALL ATTRIBUTES AND OPERATIONS IN RATIONAL ROSE

1. Right-click on the class in a diagram to make the shortcut menu visible.
2. Select the Show All Attributes menu choice to display all the attributes for the class.
3. Repeat step 1 and select the Show All Operations menu choice to display all the operations for the class.

Note: To always display the attributes and operations for a class, you can set the Show All Attributes and Show All Operations selections using the Tools:Options menu.

The class diagram called Attributes and Operations for the University Artifacts package is shown in Figure 7-6.

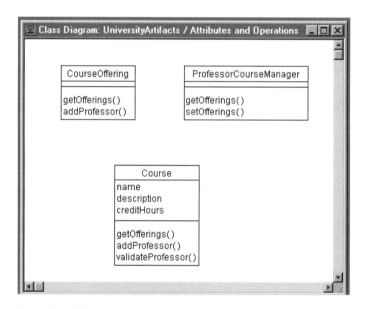

Figure 7-6   Displaying Attributes and Operations

ASSOCIATION CLASSES

A RELATIONSHIP MAY also have structure and behavior. This is true when the information deals with a link between two objects and not with one object by itself.

Consider the following example: A student may take up to four course offerings, and a course offering may have between three and ten students. Each student must receive a grade for the course offering. Where is the grade held? It doesn't belong to the student since a student will probably have different grades for different course offerings, and it doesn't belong to the course offering since a course offering has different grades for different students. The information belongs to the link between a student and a course offering. This is modeled as an association class. Since an association class behaves like any other class, it too can have relationships. Following our example, a student receives a report card each semester. This report card is made up of all the linked grade objects for the student.

CREATING ASSOCIATION CLASSES IN RATIONAL ROSE

1. Click to select the class icon from the toolbar.
2. Click on the diagram to place the class.
3. With the class selected, enter the name of the class.
4. Add the attributes and operations to the class.
5. Click to select the Link Attribute icon from the toolbar.
6. Click on the association class and drag the link attribute line to the association it modifies.
7. Create any additional relationships for the association class.

The association class Grade is shown in Figure 7-7.

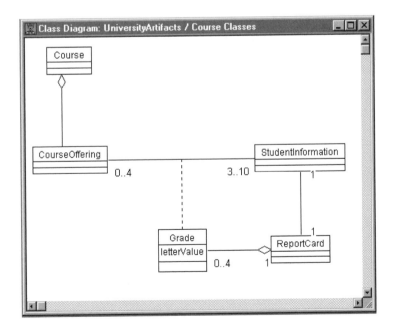

Figure 7-7 Association Class

SUMMARY

A CLASS EMBODIES a set of responsibilities that define the behavior of the objects in the class. The responsibilities are carried out by the operations defined for the class. The structure of an object is described by the attributes of the class. Each attribute is a data definition held by objects of the class. Objects defined for the class have a value for every attribute of the class. The attributes and operations defined for a class are the ones that have meaning and utility within the application that is being developed.

Messages in interaction diagrams typically are mapped to operations of the receiving class. However, there are some special cases where the message does not become an operation: messages to and from actors representing people and messages to and from classes representing GUI classes.

Many of the attributes of a class are found in the problem statement, the set of system requirements, and the flow of events documentation. They may also be discovered when supplying the definition of a class. Finally, domain expertise is also a good source of attributes for a class.

A relationship may also have structure and behavior. This is true when the information deals with a link between two objects and not with one object by itself. The structure and behavior belonging to a relationship is held in an association class.

Chapter 8

Discovering Inheritance

INHERITANCE

INHERITANCE DEFINES A relationship among classes where one class shares the structure and/or behavior of one or more classes. A hierarchy of abstractions is created in which a subclass inherits from one or more superclasses. Inheritance is also called an *is-a* or *kind-of* hierarchy. A subclass will inherit all attributes, operations, and relationships defined in any of its superclasses. Thus, attributes and operations are defined at the highest level in the hierarchy at which they are applicable, which allows all lower classes in the hierarchy to inherit them. Subclasses may be augmented with additional attributes and operations that apply only to that level of the hierarchy. A subclass may supply its own implementation of an operation. This is called polymorphism and will be discussed in Chapter 12. Since an inheritance relationship is not a relationship between different objects, the relationship is never named, role names are not used, and multiplicity does not apply.

There is no limit to the number of classes allowed in an inheritance hierarchy. However, practical experience has shown that typical C + + class hierarchies contain between three and five layers, while Smalltalk applications may be a bit deeper.

Inheritance is the key to reuse. A class can be created for one application, and then a subclass may be created to add more information needed for a different application.

There are two ways to find inheritance—generalization and specialization. Both methods typically are used for any system under development.

GENERALIZATION

GENERALIZATION PROVIDES THE capability to create superclasses that encapsulate structure and behavior common to several classes. This is very common in beginning analysis endeavors since the classes that currently exist are those that model the real world. Classes are examined for commonality of structure (attributes) and behavior (operations). For example, the StudentInformation and ProfessorInformation classes both have name, address, and phoneNumber as attributes.

You should be on the lookout for synonyms since attribute and operation names are expressed in natural language and the commonality might be hidden. Additionally, look at attributes and behavior, which at first glance may seem specific, but in reality may be generalized. For example, the StudentInformation class has an attribute called studentID, and the ProfessorInformation class has an attribute called professorID. A general attribute called userID could be created to replace the studentID and the professorID as long as the individual IDs follow the same numbering scheme (e.g., they are both four-digit numbers). If they are different (e.g., the studentID is a ten-digit alphanumeric, and the professorID is a four-digit number), then they should be kept separate.

SPECIALIZATION

SPECIALIZATION PROVIDES THE ability to create subclasses that represent refinements to the superclass—typically, structure and behavior are added to the new subclass. This method of finding inheritance often comes into play if a class already exists. Subclasses are added to specialize the behavior of an existing class. For example, the registration system could be expanded to allow senior citizens to take classes free of charge. A new subclass called SeniorCitizenInformation could be added to the UserInformation hierarchy to hold information pertinent to senior citizens.

Operations may be overridden by a subclass. This is the concept of polymorphism, which is discussed in Chapter 12. However, a subclass should never restrict an operation defined in its superclasses. That is, the subclass should never provide less behavior or structure than its superclasses.

CREATING INHERITANCE IN RATIONAL ROSE

1. Open the class diagram that will display the inheritance hierarchy.
2. Click to select the class icon from the toolbar and click on the open class diagram to draw the class.
3. With the class still selected, enter the name of the class. Note: The class could also be created in the browser and added to the open class diagram.
4. Click to select the Generalization icon on the toolbar.
5. Click on a subclass and drag the generalization line to the superclass.
6. Repeat step 5 for each additional subclass.

An inheritance relationship is shown in Figure 8-1.

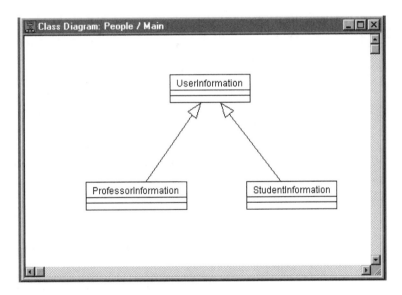

Figure 8-1   Inheritance Relationship

INHERITANCE TREES

THE BASIS FOR specialization (i.e., why subclasses were created) in an inheritance relationship is called the *discriminator.* The discriminator typically has a finite set of values, and subclasses may be created for each value. For example, one basis for discrimination for a Course class is the location of the course—OnCampusCourse and OffSiteCourse could be two subclasses of the Course class based on this discriminator. The inheritance relationship may be shown as a tree for all subclasses created from one discriminator. Another subclass of Course could be MandatoryCourse. This subclass would not be part of the inheritance tree since it belongs to a different discriminator—course type. Care must be taken when you discover multiple discriminators for a class—for example, what happens when a mandatory course is held on campus? Do you have a multiple inheritance situation? Should aggregation be used? As analysis and design progresses, the answers to these questions will lead to the structure of the model.

CREATING AN INHERITANCE TREE IN RATIONAL ROSE

1. Open the class diagram that will display the inheritance hierarchy.
2. Click to select the class icon from the toolbar and click on the open class diagram to draw the class.
3. With the class still selected, enter the name of the class. Note: The class could also be created in the browser and added to the open class diagram.
4. Click to select the Generalization icon on the toolbar.
5. Click on one subclass and drag the generalization line to the superclass.
6. For each subclass that is part of the inheritance tree, select the Generalization icon from the toolbar, click on the subclass, and drag the generalization line to the inheritance triangle.

Note: An inheritance tree may be created from two separate generalization arrows by selecting one arrow and dragging it onto the other arrow.

An inheritance tree relationship is shown in Figure 8-2.

Figure 8-2   Inheritance Tree

Attributes, operations, and relationships are relocated to the highest applicable level in the hierarchy once a superclass is created. What features should be relocated? Let's look at the UserInformation hierarchy. The attributes, operations, and relationships for the subclasses are shown in Figure 8-3. As long as name and IDNumber have the same format, they may safely be moved to the superclass (UserInformation). Both classes have a relationship to the CourseOffering class. There are two options that may be chosen for the relationships:

- Keep the relationships at the subclass level.

- Have one relationship at the superclass level with a multiplicity that includes the professor and the student objects (i.e., one CourseOffering object would be related to 4 to 11 UserInformation objects). Here a constraint stating that one UserInformation object must be a ProfessorInformation object should be added to the model.

Which way is correct? They both are. Which way is the best to use? It depends. If you have a need for a CourseOffering object to know all the students and the professor, then having one list containing this information might be handy. This would imply that the second option is the way to go. If, on the other hand, you need to know only students or professors, but not both at the same time, then the first option is probably best. It all comes down to what the system needs to do. This will be discovered by carefully examining the use cases and scenarios to discover the needed behavior.

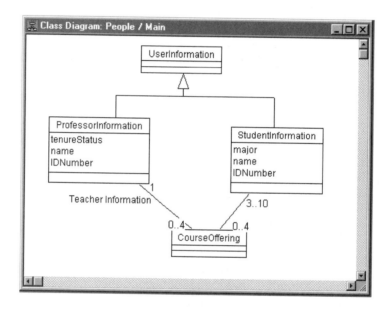

Figure 8-3   UserInformation Inheritance Hierarchy

RELOCATING ATTRIBUTES AND OPERATIONS IN RATIONAL ROSE

1. Click the + sign next to one subclass in the browser to expand the class.
2. Select the attribute or operation to be relocated.
3. Drag the attribute or operation to the superclass.
4. Delete the attribute or operation from all other subclasses.
5. Repeat steps 2 through 4 for each additional attribute or operation to be relocated.

Relocated attributes are shown in Figure 8-4.

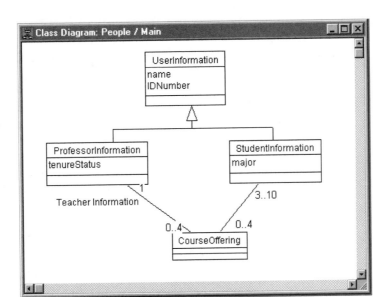

Figure 8-4   Relocated Attributes and Operations

SINGLE INHERITANCE
VERSUS MULTIPLE INHERITANCE

WITH SINGLE INHERITANCE, a class has one set of parents—that is, there is one chain of superclasses (e.g., a car is a motor vehicle that is a vehicle). Multiple inheritance involves more than one chain of superclasses (e.g., an amphibious vehicle is a motor vehicle that is a vehicle, *and* an amphibious vehicle is a water vehicle that is a vehicle). There can be numerous problems associated with multiple inheritance—for example, name clashes and multiple copies of inherited features. How the problems are overcome is very language-dependent, from the use of special features of C++ (e.g., virtual base classes), to lack of support for multiple inheritance altogether (PowerBuilder). Multiple inheritance also leads to less maintainable code—the more superclasses, the harder it is to determine what comes from where and what happens if I change something. The bottom line is: Use multiple inheritance only when it is needed, and always use it with care!

INHERITANCE VERSUS AGGREGATION

INHERITANCE IS OFTEN misused—the "inheritance is good, therefore, the more I use it, the better my code will be" syndrome. This is not true—in fact, the misuse of inheritance can lead to problems. For example, a student may be full time or part time. A StudentInformation superclass with two subclasses—FulltimeStudentInformation and ParttimeStudentInformation—could be created. Multiple problems can arise with this structure. What happens if:

- A full-time student decides to go to school only part time? This implies that an object would have to change its class.

- Another dimension is added (e.g., on scholarship, or not on scholarship)? Here you would have to add additional subclasses to model the scholarship information along with multiple inheritance to handle all the combinations (full-time student on scholarship, part-time student on scholarship, etc.).

Inheritance should be used to separate commonality from specifics. Aggregation should be used to show composite relationships. Often the two types of relationships are used together. The StudentInformation class has a classification (aggregation) that is either full time or part time (inheritance). This is shown in Figure 8-5.

SUMMARY

INHERITANCE PROVIDES THE capability to create a hierarchy of classes where common structure and behavior are shared among classes. The term superclass is the name given to the class holding the common information. The descendants are called subclasses. A subclass inherits all attributes, operations, and relationships that are defined

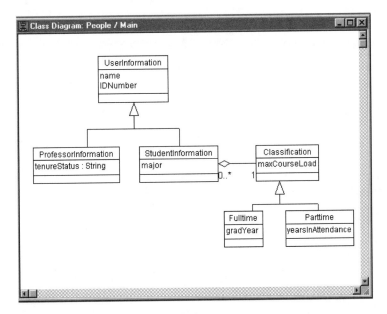

Figure 8-5   Inheritance vs. Aggregation

for all of its superclasses. There are two ways to find inheritance
in any system: generalization and specialization. Generalization
provides the ability to create superclasses to encapsulate structure
and/or behavior common to several classes. Specialization provides
the capability to create subclasses that represent refinements or addi-
tions to the structure and/or behavior specified in the superclass.

Chapter 9

Analyzing Object Behavior

MODELING DYNAMIC BEHAVIOR

USE CASES AND scenarios provide a way to describe system behavior; that is, the interaction between objects in the system. Sometimes it is necessary to look at the behavior inside an object. A state transition diagram shows the states of a single object, the events or messages that cause a transition from one state to another, and the actions that result from a state change.

A state transition diagram will not be created for every class in the system. They are created only for classes with significant dynamic behavior. Interaction diagrams can be studied to determine the dynamic objects in the system—ones receiving and sending many messages. State transition diagrams are also useful to investigate the behavior of an aggregate whole class and control classes.

Care must be taken to stay in an analysis frame of mind—concentrating on the what of the problem and not the how of the solution.

CREATING STATE TRANSITION DIAGRAMS IN RATIONAL ROSE

1. Right-click to select the class in the browser and make the shortcut menu visible.
2. Select the State Diagram menu choice. This will automatically create and open the diagram.
3. To open the diagram at another time, click the + to expand the class in the browser, and double-click on its state transition diagram in the browser.

The browser view of the state transition diagram for the CourseOffering class is shown in Figure 9-1.

Figure 9-1   State Transition Diagram in the Browser

STATES

A STATE IS a condition during the life of an object when it satisfies some condition, performs some action, or waits for an event. The state of an object may be characterized by the value of one or more of the attributes of the class. For example, a CourseOffering object may be open (able to add a student) or closed (maximum number of students already assigned to the CourseOffering object). The state depends upon the number of students assigned to the particular CourseOffering object. Additionally, a state of an object may be characterized by the existence of a link to another object. A professor may be teaching or on sabbatical. This depends upon the existence of a link to a CourseOffering object. Looking at the state of an object can validate the multiplicity chosen for a relationship to another object. That is, if being in a state depends upon the existence of a link to another object, this implies that the multiplicity of the relationship modifying the role of the associated class must include 0 (i.e., the relationship is optional). Thus, the states of an object are found by examining the attributes and links defined for the object.

The UML notation for a state is a rectangle with rounded corners, as shown in Figure 9-2.

Figure 9-2   UML Notation for a State

A state transition diagram encompasses all the messages that an object can send and receive. Scenarios represent one path through a state transition diagram. The interval between two messages sent by an object typically represents a state. Therefore, sequence diagrams may be examined to discover the states for an object (look at the space between the lines representing messages received by the object). If we had created sequence diagrams for each use case in the ESU Course Registration system, we would discover that objects in the CourseOffering class can be in one of the following states: Initialization (created prior to registration, but students have not been added to it), Open (able to accept students), Closed (maximum number of students already registered for it), or Canceled (no longer offered).

CREATING STATES IN RATIONAL ROSE
1. Click to select the state icon from the toolbar.
2. Click to place the state on the state transition diagram.
3. With the state still selected, enter the name of the state.

The states of the CourseOffering class are shown in Figure 9-3.

STATE TRANSITIONS

A STATE TRANSITION represents a change from an originating state to a successor state (that may be the same as the originating state). An action can accompany a state transition.

There are two ways to transition out of a state—automatic and nonautomatic. An automatic state transition occurs when the activity of the originating state completes—there is no named event associated with the state transition. A nonautomatic state transition is

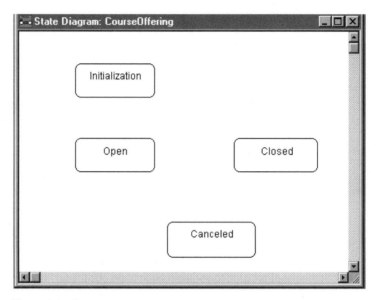

Figure 9-3   States

caused by a named event (either from another object or from outside the system). Both types of state transitions are considered to take zero time and cannot be interrupted. A state transition is represented by an arrow that points from the originating state to the successor state.

CREATING STATE TRANSITIONS IN RATIONAL ROSE

1. Click to select the state transition icon from the toolbar.
2. Click to select the originating state on the state transition diagram.
3. Drag the state transition to the successor state.
4. If the state transition is a named transition, enter the name while the state transition arrow is still selected.

State transitions are shown in Figure 9-4.

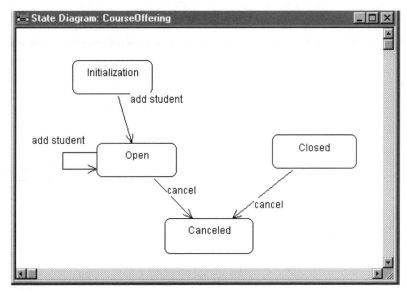

Figure 9-4   State Transitions

SPECIAL STATES

THERE ARE TWO special states that are added to the state transition diagram. The first is a start state. Each diagram must have one and only one start state since the object must be in a consistent state when it is created. The UML notation for a start state is a small solid-filled circle, as shown in Figure 9-5. The second special state is a stop state. An object can have multiple stop states. The UML notation for a stop state is a bull's-eye, as shown in Figure 9-5.

Figure 9-5   UML Notation for Start and Stop States

CREATING START STATES IN RATIONAL ROSE

1. Click to select the start icon from the toolbar.
2. Click on the state transition diagram to draw the start icon.
3. Click to select the state transition icon from the toolbar.
4. Click on the start icon and drag the arrow to the desired state.

A start state is shown in Figure 9-6.

Figure 9-6   Start State

CREATING STOP STATES IN RATIONAL ROSE

1. Select the stop icon from the toolbar.
2. Click on the state transition diagram to draw the stop icon.
3. Select the state transition icon from the bar.
4. Click on the state and drag the arrow to the stop icon.

A stop state is shown in Figure 9-7.

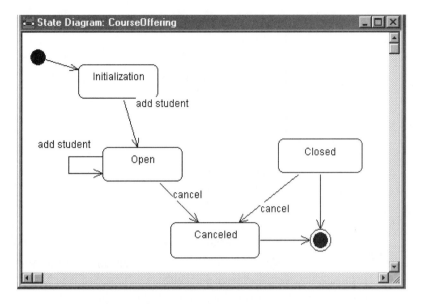

Figure 9-7   Stop State

STATE TRANSITION DETAILS

A STATE TRANSITION may have an action and/or a guard condition
associated with it, and may also trigger an event. An action is the
behavior that occurs when the state transition occurs. An event is
a message that is sent to another object in the system. A guard condition is a Boolean expression of attribute values that allows a state
transition only if the condition is true. Both actions and guards are
behaviors of the object and typically become operations. Often these
operations are private—that is, they are used only by the object itself.
The UML notation for state transition detailed information is shown
in Figure 9-8.

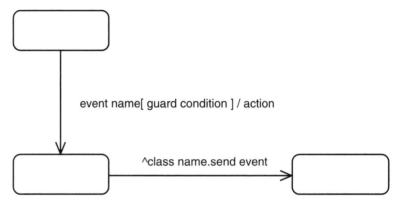

Figure 9-8   UML Notation for State Transition Details

ADDING STATE TRANSITION DETAILS IN RATIONAL ROSE

1. Right-click on the state transition arrow to make the shortcut menu visible.
2. Select the Specification menu choice.
3. Select the Detail tab.
4. Enter the action, guard, and/or the event to be sent.
5. Click the OK button to close the specification.

A state transition detail is shown in Figure 9-9.

STATE DETAILS

ACTIONS THAT ACCOMPANY all state transitions into a state may be placed as an entry action within the state. Likewise, actions that accompany all state transitions out of a state may be placed as exit actions within the state. Behavior that occurs within the state is called an activity. An activity starts when the state is entered and either completes or is interrupted by an outgoing state transition. The behavior may be a simple action, or it may be an event sent

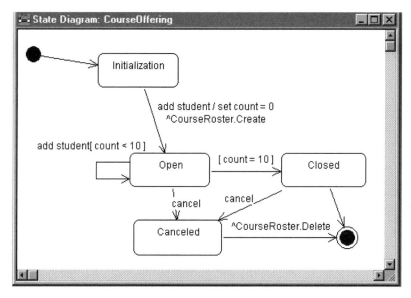

Figure 9-9   State Transition Details

to another object. As with actions and guards, this behavior typically
is mapped to operations on the object. The UML notation for state
detailed information is shown in Figure 9-10.

Figure 9-10   State Details

CREATING ENTRY ACTIONS, EXIT ACTIONS,
AND ACTIVITIES IN RATIONAL ROSE

1. Right-click on the state to make the shortcut menu visible.
2. Select the Specification menu choice.
3. Select the Detail tab.
4. Right-click on the Action field to make the shortcut menu visible.
5. Select the Insert menu choice. This will create an action called entry.
6. Double-click on entry to make the Action Specification visible.
7. Select the type of action—simple or send event.
8. Enter the action or send event information.
9. Select when the action should occur: on entry, on exit, entry until exit, or upon event.
10. Click the OK button to close the Action Specification.
11. Click the OK button to close the State Specification.

A state with detailed information is shown in Figure 9-11.

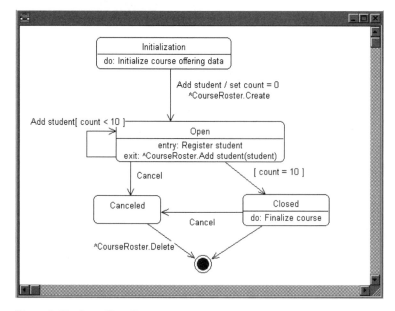

Figure 9-11   State Details

SUMMARY

CLASSES THAT EXHIBIT significant dynamic behavior are analyzed further by creating state transition diagrams. This type of diagram shows all the states of an object, the events that the object receives, and the resulting actions that are taken. State transition events, along with their accompanying actions, are considered to take zero time and cannot be interrupted. States, along with their accompanying activities, can be interrupted.

.

Chapter 10

Checking the Model

WHY HOMOGENIZE?

ACCORDING TO *Webster's New Collegiate Dictionary,* the word *homogenize* means to blend into a smooth mixture, to make homogeneous. As more use cases and scenarios are developed, it is necessary to make the model homogeneous. This is especially true if multiple teams are working on different parts of the model. Since use cases and scenarios deal with the written word, people may use different words to mean the same thing, or they may interpret words differently. At this time, classes may be combined, classes may be split into multiple classes, or a class may be eliminated from the model. This is just the natural maturation of the model during the project life cycle.

Homogenization does not happen at one point in the life cycle—it *must* be ongoing. Projects that wait until the end to gather information developed by multiple groups of people are doomed to failure. I have found that the most successful projects are made up of teams that have constant communication mechanisms employed. Communication may be as simple as a phone call or as formal as a scheduled meeting—it all depends on the project and the nature of the need to talk (for example, is it a simple question or a formal review of a piece of the system?). The only thing that matters is the fact that the teams are not working in isolation.

COMBINING CLASSES

IF DIFFERENT TEAMS are working on different scenarios, a class may be called by different names. The name conflicts must be resolved. This is accomplished mainly through model walk-throughs. Each class, along with its definition, is examined. Also examine the attributes and operations defined for the classes. Look for the use of synonyms. Once it has been determined that two classes are doing the same thing, choose the class with the name that is closest to the language used by the customers.

Pay careful attention to the control classes created for the system. Initially, one control class is allocated per use case. This might be overkill. Control classes with similar behavior may be combined. Examine the sequencing logic in the control classes for the system. If it is very similar, the control classes may be combined into one control class.

In the ESU Course Registration System, there is a control class for the *Maintain Course Information* use case and one for the *Create Course Catalog* use case. Each control class gets information from a boundary class and deals with course information. It is possible that these two control classes could be combined since they have similar behavior and access similar information.

SPLITTING CLASSES

CLASSES SHOULD BE examined to determine if they are following the golden rule of OO, which states that a class should do one thing and do it really well. They should be cohesive; for example, a StudentInformation class that contains information about the Student actor as well as information about what courses the student has successfully completed is doing too much. This is better modeled as two classes—StudentInformation and Transcript, with an association between them.

Often, what appears to be only an attribute ends up having structure and behavior unto itself and should be split off into its own class. For an example, we'll look at Departments in the University. Each Course is sponsored by a Department. Initially, this information was modeled as an attribute of the Course class. Further analysis showed that it was necessary to capture the number of students taking classes in each department, the number of professors that teach department courses, and the number of courses offered by each department. Hence, a Department class was created. The initial attribute of Department for a Course was replaced with an association between Course and Department.

ELIMINATING CLASSES

A CLASS MAY be eliminated altogether from the model. This happens when:

- The class does not have any structure or behavior
- The class does not participate in any use cases

In particular, examine control classes. Lack of sequencing responsibility may lead to the deletion of the control class. This is especially true if the control class is only a pass-through—that is, the control class receives information from a boundary class and immediately passes it to an entity class without the need for sequencing logic.

In the ESU Course Registration System, initially we would create a control class for the *Select Courses to Teach* use case. This use case provides the capability for professors to state what course offerings they will teach for a given semester. There is no sequencing logic needed for the control class—the professor enters the information on the GUI screen, and the professor is added to the selected offering. Here is a case where the control class for the use case could be eliminated.

CONSISTENCY CHECKING

CONSISTENCY CHECKING IS needed since the static view of the system, as shown in class diagrams, and the dynamic view of the system, as shown in use case diagrams and interaction diagrams, are under development in parallel. Since both views are under development concurrently, they must be cross-checked to ensure that different assumptions or decisions are not being made in different views.

Consistency checking does not occur during a separate phase or a single step of the analysis process. It should be integrated throughout the life cycle of the system under development.

Consistency checking is best accomplished by forming a small team (five to six people, at most) to do the work. The team should be composed of a cross section of personnel—analysts and designers, customers or customer representatives, domain experts, and test personnel.

SCENARIO WALK-THROUGH

A PRIMARY METHOD of consistency checking is to walk through the high-risk scenarios as represented by a sequence or collaboration diagram. Since each message represents behavior of the receiving class, verify that each message is captured as an operation on the class diagram. Verify that two interacting objects have a pathway for communication via either an association or an aggregation. Especially check for reflexive relationships that may be needed since these relationships are easy to miss during analysis. Reflexive relationships are needed when multiple objects of the same class interact during a scenario.

For each class represented on the class diagram, make sure the class participates in at least one scenario. For each operation listed for a class, verify that either the operation is used in at least one scenario or that it is needed for completeness. Finally, verify that each object included in a sequence or collaboration diagram belongs to a class on the class diagram.

EVENT TRACING

FOR EVERY MESSAGE shown in a sequence or collaboration diagram, verify that an operation on the sending class is responsible for sending the event and that an operation on the receiving class expects the event and handles it. Verify that there is an association or aggregation on the class diagram between the sending and receiving classes. Add the relationship to the class diagram if it is missing. Finally, if a state transition diagram for the class exists, verify that the event is represented on the diagram for the receiving class. This is needed since the diagram shows all the events that a class may receive.

DOCUMENTATION REVIEW

EACH CLASS SHOULD be documented: Check for uniqueness of class names and review all definitions for completeness. Ensure that all attributes and operations have a complete definition. Finally, check that all standards, format specifications, and content rules established for the project have been followed.

SUMMARY

AS MORE USE cases and scenarios are developed, it is necessary to make the model homogeneous. This is especially true if multiple teams are working on different parts of the model. Classes are examined to determine if:

- Two or more classes may be combined
- One class should be split
- A class should be eliminated altogether

Consistency checking must be performed throughout the life cycle of any project. Consistency checking is needed because several views of the system are under development in parallel and care must be taken to ensure that the models stay in synch. There are three ways to perform consistency checking: scenario walk-throughs, event tracing, and review of the model documentation.

Chapter 11

Designing the
System Architecture

THE NEED FOR ARCHITECTURE

OVER THE YEARS, I have heard many definitions of software architecture that range from "software architecture is what software architects do" to "software architecture is politics." I have come to the conclusion that software architecture is very difficult to define. It is a range of artifacts that is used to specify the strategic decisions about the structure and behavior of the system, the collaborations among the system elements, and the physical deployment of the system.

"Establishing a sound architectural foundation is absolutely essential to the success of an object-oriented project. Some teams try to ignore this phase, either because they are in such a rush to get a product out quickly they feel they don't have time to architect, or because they don't believe that architecting provides them any real value. Either way, the resulting head-long rush to code is always disastrous: fail to carry out this step properly, and your project will likely experience software meltdown."[1]

Architecture development is a very complicated issue. The architecture of the system is developed iteratively in the elaboration phase of development. "The architecture of a proposed system does not appear in a flash. It takes exploration of the use cases, a proof-of-concept prototype, an architectural baseline, and other efforts during the Inception and Elaboration phases."[2] Executable prototypes of the architecture are built to verify that the design decisions made are correct. "Building something executable is absolutely essential, because it forces the development team to validate their design assumptions in the harsh light of reality."[3]

---

[1] Booch, Grady. *Object Solutions*. Redwood City, CA: Addison-Wesley, 1995.

[2] Jacobson, Ivar. *The Objector Software Development Process,* Draft Edition.

[3] *Ibid.*

THE ARCHITECTURE TEAM

EACH PROJECT SHOULD have a chief architect who may be assisted by a small team of people. "The main activities of the architect include the definition of the architecture of the software, the maintenance of the architectural integrity of the software, the assessment of the technical risks of the project, the definition of the order and content of the successive iterations along with the planning of each iteration, providing consulting to various design, implementation, integration, and quality assurance teams and assisting in providing future market directions."[4]

THE "4 + 1" VIEW OF ARCHITECTURE

SOFTWARE ARCHITECTURE IS not a one-dimensional thing—it is made up of concurrent multiple views. Figure 11-1 shows the different views of software architecture.[5] The rest of this chapter addresses the elements in each view of the architecture, along with the UML notation used to represent the architectural decisions made for the system.

THE LOGICAL VIEW

THIS VIEW OF architecture addresses the functional requirements of the system—what the system should provide in terms of services to its users. The logical architecture is captured in class diagrams that contain the classes and relationships that represent the key abstractions of the system under development. Most of the UML notation that has been addressed so far is contained within this view of architecture (e.g., classes, associations, aggregations, generalization, and packages).

---

[4] Kruchten, Philippe. *Software Architecture and Iterative Development.* Santa Clara, CA: Rational Software Corporation. P. 53. April 1994.

[5] *Ibid.*

Figure 11-1   The "4 + 1" View of Architecture

This view of architecture is addressed early in the elaboration phase with the creation of classes and packages that represent the major abstractions of the domain. As time moves on, more classes and packages are added to the model to reflect the decisions made concerning the key mechanisms of the system. A key mechanism is a decision regarding common standards, policies, and practices. The selection of the key mechanisms for a system is often referred to as tactical design. "Poor tactical design can ruin even the most profound architecture, and so the team must mitigate this risk by explicitly identifying the project's key policies."[6] Some common key mechanisms involve the selection of an implementation language, persistent data storage, the look and feel of the user interface, error handling, communication mechanisms, object distribution and migration, and networking.

Today, many patterns exist that may be used to implement the key mechanism decisions made for your system. I strongly recommend looking into patterns before you try to "roll your own."

---

[6] Booch, Grady. *Object Solutions*. Redwood City, CA: Addison-Wesley, 1995.

Additionally, the concepts of cohesion, closure, and reuse will affect the choices that you make. Robert Martin discusses some of the ramifications of the choice of packages for your system in his book, *Designing Object-Oriented C++ Applications Using the Booch Method.* Although this book uses the Booch notation and process, it is still applicable to the Rational Objectory Process and the UML. The bottom line is: The UML may be used to communicate the strategic decisions made for your system by adding packages and classes to the model to communicate, implement, and document these decisions.

Sample Key Mechanisms for the ESU Course Registration Problem

Since most of the development team had prior experience using the C++ language, and because this system eventually will be expanded to include other university functionality, C++ is the language of choice by the architecture team. The architecture team also decided that a particular set of graphical user interface (GUI) controls should be used to control the look and feel of the user interface, and therefore, a package called GUI Controls was added to the model. The database persistence strategy chosen by the architecture team is the use of a corresponding database class (shadow class) for each persistent class in the system. Although other strategies that mainly involve the use of inheritance could have been chosen by the team, this strategy was chosen due to the fact that expertise in implementing this method of persistence already existed and the team felt that it had the least amount of risk. A database package containing the shadow classes was added to the model at this time. Additionally, it was decided to make use of the C++ features of catch and throw for exceptions. Rather than have each class be responsible for knowing how to catch and throw exceptions, a package called Error Handling was added to the model. Finally, a set of commercial foundation classes was chosen for this system. The packages representing the key mechanism decisions made for the course registration system are shown in Figure 11-2.

Since the Error Handling package and the Foundations package are used by every other package in the system, they are global packages.

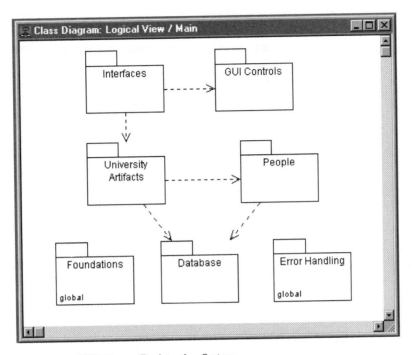

Figure 11-2   ESU Course Registration System

MAKING A PACKAGE GLOBAL IN RATIONAL ROSE

1. Right-click to select the package on a class diagram.
2. Select the Specification menu choice.
3. Select the Detail tab.
4. Click to select the global checkbox.
5. Click the OK button to close the specification.

THE COMPONENT VIEW

THIS VIEW OF architecture concerns itself with the actual software module organization within the development environment. The component view of architecture takes into account derived requirements related to ease of development, software management, reuse, and constraints imposed by programming languages and development tools. The modeling elements in the component view of architecture are packages and components along with their connections.

A package in this view of architecture represents a physical partitioning of the system. Component view packages are often called subsystems. The packages are organized in a hierarchy of layers where each layer has a well-defined interface. The fact that an object-oriented system tends to be a layered system should not bring any surprises. This is due to the definition of an object— it should do one thing, and do it well! A drawing showing some typical layers of a system can be found in Figure 11-3.

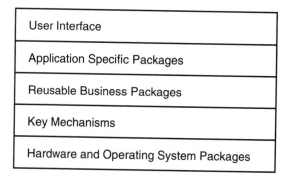

Figure 11-3   System Layers

The UML notation for a package in the component view is the same as a package in the logical view—a notched folder, as found in Figure 11-4.

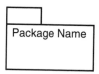

Figure 11-4   UML Notation for a Package

CREATING COMPONENT VIEW PACKAGES IN RATIONAL ROSE

1. Right-click to select the Component View package on the browser and make the shortcut menu visible.
2. Select the New:Package menu choice. This will add an item called NewPackage to the browser.
3. With the NewPackage still selected, enter the name of the package.

The main component diagram typically is a view of the packages (subsystems) defined for the system.

 THE MAIN COMPONENT DIAGRAM IN RATIONAL ROSE

1. Double-click on the Main Diagram under the Component View package on the browser to open the diagram.
2. Click to select a package and drag the package onto the diagram.
3. Repeat step 2 for each additional package.
4. Dependency relationships are added by selecting the dependency icon from the toolbar, clicking on the package representing the client, and dragging the arrow to the package representing the supplier.

The main component diagram for the ESU Course Registration problem is shown in Figure 11-5.

Information in the logical view of the model is connected to information in the component view of the model by mapping logical view packages to component view packages. In general, a logical view package corresponds directly to a physical view package. However, there are times where a one-to-one mapping is not possible. Some reasons for this are: a logical package may be divided for implementation purposes (possibly developed by different contractors); logical packages may be merged to keep closely communicating objects together; and, finally, physical view packages may be added to implement low-level functionality not represented during analysis (i.e., communication for distributed systems).

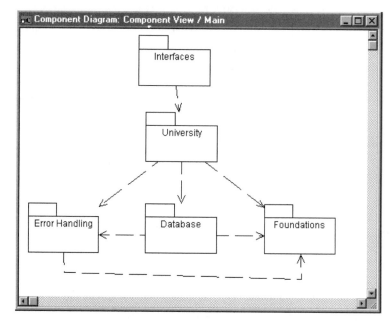

Figure 11-5   Main Component Diagram

The mapping of logical packages to component packages for the ESU Course Registration problem is straightforward, and is shown in Table 11-1.

Component Package	Logical Package(s)
Interfaces	Interfaces, GUI Controls
University	UniversityArtifacts, People
Database	Database
Foundations	Foundations
Error Handling	Error Handling

Table 11-1   Mapping of Logical Packages to Component Packages

**MAPPING LOGICAL PACKAGES TO
COMPONENT PACKAGES IN RATIONAL ROSE**

1. Right-click to select the component package on the browser and make the shortcut menu visible.
2. Select the Specification menu choice.
3. Select the Packages tab.
4. Right-click to select the logical package and make the shortcut menu visible.
5. Select the Assign menu choice.
6. Click the OK button to close the Specification.

The mapping of logical packages to component packages for the ESU Course Registration problem is shown in Figure 11-6.

Figure 11-6   Logical to Component Package Mappings

Source Code Components

In the component view of the model, a component represents a software file that is contained by a package (subsystem). The type of file is language dependent (e.g., in C + +, software components represent .h and .cpp files, in Java they represent .java files, and in PowerBuilder, a software component is a .pbl). Classes in the logical view are mapped to components in the component view. In C++, the mapping is typically one-to-one; that is, one class maps to one component. However, there are times that more than one class will be mapped to a component. This is usually done when there is very tight coupling between the classes. For example, a container and its iterator are contained within one .h and one .cpp file. In this case, the container and the iterator classes would be mapped to one component. I have also seen classes that represent a pattern of collaboration mapped to one physical file. The UML notation for a component is shown in Figure 11-7.

Figure 11-7   UML Notation for a Component

Software Components in the
ESU Course Registration Problem

This is a relatively simple system, and the decision was made to provide a one-to-one mapping between classes and components—each class has its own header and .cpp file.

CREATING COMPONENTS IN RATIONAL ROSE

1. Open a component diagram.
2. Click to select the Package Specification icon on the toolbar.
3. Click on the diagram to place the component. This will also add the component to the Browser.
4. While the component is still selected, enter the name of the component.

A sample component diagram is shown in Figure 11-8.

Figure 11-8   Software Components

MAPPING CLASSES TO COMPONENTS IN RATIONAL ROSE

1. Right-click to select the component on the browser and make the shortcut menu visible.
2. Select the Specification menu choice.
3. Select the Classes tab.
4. Right-click to select the class and make the shortcut menu visible.
5. Select the Assign menu choice.
6. Click the OK button to close the Specification.

The browser view of the mapping of classes to components for the ESU Course Registration System is shown in Figure 11-9.

Figure 11-9   Mapping Classes to Components

THE PROCESS VIEW

THIS VIEW OF architecture focuses on the run-time implementation structure of the system. The process view of architecture takes into account requirements such as performance, reliability, scalability, integrity, system management, and synchronization. Components are also used in this view of architecture. Component diagrams are created to view the run-time and executable components created for the system. Components are related via dependency relationships. Run-time components show the mapping of classes to run-time libraries such as Java applets, ActiveX components, and dynamic libraries. Executable components show the interfaces and calling dependencies among executables.

In Rational Rose, the information for the process view of architecture is created as diagrams in the Component View of the tool. Components (either run-time or executable) are added to the package representing their own subsystem. Diagrams are created to show dependencies between the different types of components in the system.

For the ESU Course Registration System, the architecture team
decided that there would be two DLLs—one containing course and
course-offering information, and one containing database information. This allocation was chosen since it was felt that the course
structure and the choice of database strategy was subject to change.
By making them libraries, only the libraries would have to be
replaced to implement future changes. There are three executables
for the system—one for the Registrar to create and maintain the system, one for the Student to access the system, and one for the Professor to access the system. There is no communication between the
executables. The component diagram for the Professor executable
(professor.exe) is shown in Figure 11-10.

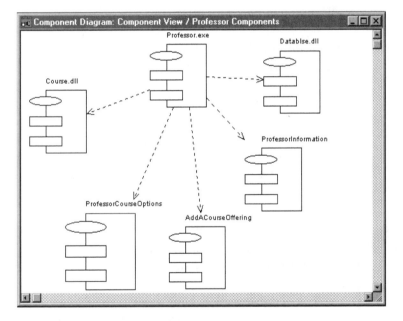

Figure 11-10   Professor Executable

THE DEPLOYMENT VIEW

THIS VIEW OF architecture involves mapping software to processing
nodes—it shows the configuration of run-time processing elements
and the software processes living in them. The deployment view

takes into account requirements such as system availability, reliability, performance, and scalability. Deployment diagrams are created to show the different nodes along with their connections in the system. The deployment diagram visualizes the distribution of components across the enterprise. Run-time processing elements are represented as nodes. Nodes are connected by associations indicating communication paths between them. Software processes are illustrated as text attached to a node or group of nodes.

This diagram allows the architecture team to understand the system topology and aids in mapping subsystems to executable processes. Issues such as processor architecture, speed, and capacity, along with interprocess communication bandwidth/capacity, physical location of the hardware, and distributed processing techniques all come into play.

Deployment Diagram for the ESU Course Registration System

After studying the component packages (subsystems) defined for the problem, examining existing hardware, and estimating the load on the system during the course registration period, the architecture team decided that they will need five processors for the system—one to handle the professor executable, one for the database, and three for student registration.

CREATING THE DEPLOYMENT DIAGRAM IN RATIONAL ROSE

1. Rose automatically creates the deployment diagram. To open the diagram, double-click on the Deployment Diagram on the browser.
2. To create a node, click to select the Processor icon, and click on the diagram to place the node.
3. With the node still selected, enter the name of the node.
4. To create a connection between nodes, click to select the connection icon from the toolbar, click on one node on the deployment diagram, and drag the connection to the other node.

The deployment diagram for the ESU Course Registration problem is shown in Figure 11-11.

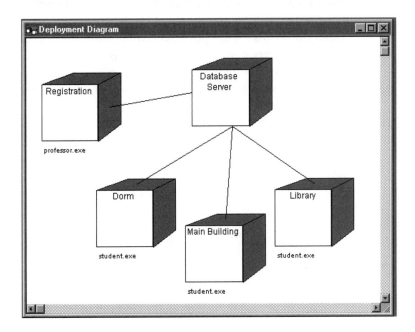

Figure 11-11   Deployment Diagram

THE USE CASE VIEW

THIS VIEW OF architecture demonstrates and validates the logical, process, component, and deployment views. Sequence diagrams and collaboration diagrams are created to show how the various design elements interact to produce the desired behavior.

SUMMARY

SOFTWARE ARCHITECTURE IS not one-dimensional—it is made up of concurrent multiple views—logical, component, process, and deployment. Scenarios are developed to validate the different views. Good architectures are constructed in well-defined layers

of abstraction where there is a clear separation between the interface
and implementation of each layer. Key mechanisms focus on decisions regarding common standards, policies, and practices. Packages
are created to show the architectural layout of the system. Architecture also addresses the physical layout of the system. Component
diagrams are created to show subsystems that are the physical implementations of the logical packages. Deployment diagrams are created to show the hardware configuration that is used for the system
under development.

Chapter 12

Building the Iterations

THE ITERATION PLANNING PROCESS

THE ITERATION RELEASE plan prescribes schedules for all the increments of the system. "Such a plan must identify a controlled series of architectural releases, each growing in its functionality and ultimately encompassing the requirements of the complete production system."[1]

"The iteration plan must state the iteration specific goals:

- Capabilities being developed
- Risks being mitigated during this iteration
- Defects being fixed during the iteration

Exit criteria:

- Updated capability information
- Updated risk mitigation plan
- A release description document, which captures the results of an iteration
- Test cases and results of the tests conducted on the products including a list of defects
- An iteration plan, detailing the next iteration including measurable evaluation criteria for assessing the results of the next iteration(s)"[2]

The scenarios developed during analysis are the main input to this phase of development. The scenarios are examined and prioritized according to risk, importance to the customer, and the need to develop certain basic scenarios first. This task is best accomplished with a team made up of a domain expert, analysts, the architect, and testing personnel. "Scenarios should be grouped so that for each release, they collectively provide a meaningful chunk of the

---

[1] Booch, Grady. *Object Solutions*. Redwood City, CA: Addison-Wesley, 1995.

[2] Kruchten, Philippe. *A Rational Development Process*. Santa Clara, CA: Rational Software Corporation. Available at www.rational.com.

system's behavior and additionally require the development team to attack the project's next highest risks."[3] As each iteration is completed, risks are re-evaluated and the project plan is updated as needed. "For most projects, plan on about five (plus or minus two) intermediate releases."[4]

The iteration planning process is shown in Figure 12-1.

Figure 12-1   Iteration Planning Process

ESU Course Registration Problem Iteration Plan
For the ESU Course Registration problem, the iteration plan is:

- Iteration 1
    Maintain professor information
    Select courses to teach
    Maintain curriculum

- Iteration 2
    Maintain student information
    Generate catalog

- Iteration 3
    Register for courses
    Request class roster

---

[3] Booch, Grady. *Object Solutions.* Redwood City, CA: Addison-Wesley, 1995.

[4] *Ibid.*

Iteration 1 addresses the database risk—the courses must be stored in a database that is accessible to all. The *Maintain Professor Info* and *Select Courses to Teach* scenarios are in this iteration since they must be completed before the catalog can be generated. Iteration 2 adds the functionality needed to register a student (the student information must be in the database, and the catalog must be available for the students). Iteration 3 completes the system.

DESIGNING THE USER INTERFACE

EARLIER IN THE project life cycle, placeholder classes were created for the boundary classes for the system. Now these classes must be finalized—number of windows, window layout, and handling events from users. Sequence diagrams are good sources for user interface requirements. Something in the user interface must provide the capability to receive all messages coming from an actor. Something in the user interface must provide the capability to send all messages going to an actor.

Select Courses to Teach User Interface Design

The scenarios dealing with the *Select Courses to Teach* use case were examined, and the following requirements were found:

- The professor must enter a password to enter the system. A window prompting the professor for a password was created.

- If the password is valid, the ProfessorCourseOptions window is displayed. The ProfessorCourseOptions window contains a field for the semester and the following buttons: ADD COURSE, DELETE COURSE, REVIEW SCHEDULE, PRINT SCHEDULE.

- Windows for the addition, deletion, and review options were created.

This book concentrates on the design of the ADD COURSE option for the scenario. It is important to note that the design of the system cannot be based on only one scenario—the design matures as more scenarios are developed. I have chosen to use one scenario to illustrate the Rational Objectory Design Process and the UML notation that may be used to communicate the design decisions.

The ADD COURSE option deals with adding a professor to a course offering as the teacher. This scenario needs a window to allow the professor to input the needed information—I call it the Addition window. The Addition window contains the following selections:

- Course name field

- Course number field

- Course offerings scroll box

- OK button

- Cancel button

- Quit button

Once the professor enters the course name and number, the system will retrieve and display the course offerings. Additionally, the professor will be able to select an offering. When the OK button is pushed, a message is sent to the course object.

The actual implementation of the GUI depends upon the class library chosen and is beyond the scope of this book. This section was included so you would understand the implications of object-oriented GUI design. Most GUI design is accomplished via a GUI builder. In this case, once the classes are created, the Analyzer may be used to reverse engineer the GUI code and update the model.

ADDING DESIGN CLASSES

CLASSES ARE TYPICALLY added to the model to facilitate the *how* of a system. For example, the course registration system states that a professor must enter a password, which must be validated. A class that knows how to validate passwords is added to the system so this requirement may be implemented. As classes are added to the system, they are displayed on diagrams as needed.

An updated class diagram for the ESU Course Registration problem is shown in Figure 12-2.

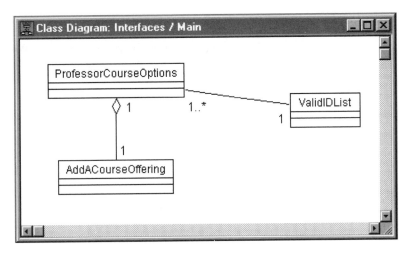

Figure 12-2   Design Level Class

THE EMERGENCE OF PATTERNS

DESIGN PATTERNS PROVIDE solutions to common software design problems. Thus, design patterns may play a part in designing the how of a system. In the words of Grady Booch, "patterns are, well, *very cool.*"[5] Patterns provide the capability to reuse successful designs and architectures, which leads to more maintainable systems and increased productivity. As with any classes developed at this point in the life cycle, the classes created to instantiate the design pattern are added to the model and to class diagrams. For example, the Abstract Factory pattern may be used to create the different types of UserInformation objects needed. Today there are many books published with descriptions of design patterns. One of the most popular books is *Design Patterns: Elements of Reusable Object-Oriented Software* by E. Gamma, et al., published by Addison-Wesley in 1995.

---

[5] Booch, Grady. *Best of Booch.* SIGS Reference Library, New York, NY, 1996. Page 167.

DESIGNING RELATIONSHIPS

THE FOLLOWING DESIGN decisions must be made for relationships: navigation, containment, refinement, and multiplicity implementation.

Navigation

Associations and aggregations are bidirectional relationships. During design, associations are revisited to determine if bidirectionality is indeed needed. If possible, the relationship is made unidirectional (i.e., navigable in only one direction) since unidirectional relationships are easier to implement and maintain.

SETTING NAVIGATION IN RATIONAL ROSE

1. Right-click at the end of the association or aggregation line to be made non-navigable to make the shortcut menu visible.
2. Click to toggle the Navigation menu choice.

A unidirectional association (Course can navigate to Course-Offering, but CourseOffering cannot navigate to Course) is shown in Figure 12-3.

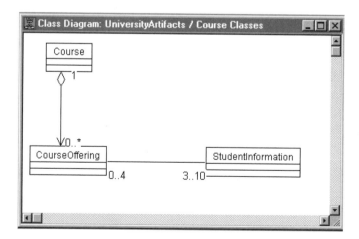

Figure 12-3   Navigation

Containment

Aggregation containment must also be added to the model. Containment may be by value or by reference. Containment by value implies exclusive ownership by the containing class and is shown by a filled diamond. Containment by reference does not mandate exclusive ownership; it is shown by an open diamond.

SETTING AGGREGATION CONTAINMENT IN RATIONAL ROSE

1. Right-click on the aggregation diamond to make the shortcut menu visible.
2. Select the desired containment—By Value or By Reference.

A containment by value relationship (ProfessorCourseOptions contains AddACourseOffering) and a containment by reference relationship (ProfessorCourseOptions to ValidIDList) are shown in Figure 12-4.

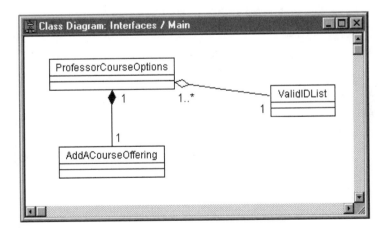

Figure 12-4   Containment

Refinement

An association relationship may be changed into a dependency relationship at this time. A dependency relationship implies that the object requesting the service (client) of another object (supplier) does

not have intrinsic knowledge of the location of the supplier object—
it must be told where the object is located. Typically, the supplier
object is passed as a parameter to one of the methods of the client
class, or it is declared locally within a method of the client class. A
dependency relationship is shown by a dashed arrow pointing from
the client to the supplier.

CREATING DEPENDENCY RELATIONSHIPS IN RATIONAL ROSE

1. Click to select the dependency relationship icon on the
   toolbar.
2. Click on the class playing the role of the client.
3. Drag the dependency relationship line to the class playing
   the role of the supplier.

A dependency relationship between CourseOffering and
DBCourseOffering is shown in Figure 12-5.

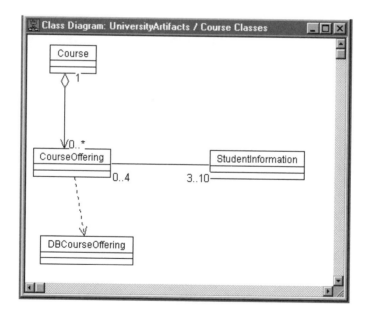

Figure 12-5   Dependency Relationship

Multiplicity Implementation

Multiplicity of one is implemented as an embedded object, a reference, or a pointer. Multiplicity of more than one is typically implemented using a container class (e.g., a set or list). Again, the list may be an embedded object or a pointer to the container. The decision to update the model to show all the containers that are being used is a tool/project issue. I typically do not show all the containers since they tend to clutter a diagram—instead I use the code generation properties of Rose to set the correct container. I have included the diagram and instructions on how to create parameterized and instantiated parameterized classes only as an illustration.

CREATING PARAMETERIZED CLASSES IN RATIONAL ROSE

1. Click to select the Parameterized class icon from the toolbar. You may have to add this icon to the toolbar using the Customize option.
2. Click on a class diagram to place the parameterized class.
3. While the parameterized class is still selected, enter its name.
4. Right-click to select the class in the Browser or on a class diagram.
5. Select the Specification menu choice.
6. Select the Detail tab.
7. Right-click on the Formal Arguments field to make the pop-up menu visible.
8. Select the Insert menu choice, which will insert a formal argument with a name of argname and a type of argtype.
9. With the argname selected, enter the name of the formal argument.
10. Click to select the argtype and enter the type of the formal argument.
11. Repeat steps 7 through 10 for each argument.
12. Click the OK button to close the Specification.

CREATING INSTANTIATED PARAMETERIZED
CLASSES IN RATIONAL ROSE

1. Click to select the class icon on the toolbar.
2. Click on the class diagram to place the class.
3. With the class still selected, select the Edit:Change Into:Instantiated Class menu choice.
4. Right-click on the instantiated class to make the pop-up menu visible.
5. Select the Specification menu choice.
6. Select the Detail tab.
7. Right-click on the Actual Arguments field to make the pop-up menu visible.
8. Select the Insert menu choice, which will add an argument with name = argname and type = argtype.
9. With the argname still selected, enter the name of the argument.
10. Click to select the argtype and blank it out.
11. Repeat steps 7 through 10 for each actual argument.
12. Click the OK button to close the Specification.
13. Click to select the Dependency icon from the toolbar.
14. Draw a dependency relationship between the instantiated class and the parameterized class.
15. Add relationships to the instantiated class as needed.

A parameterized class and an instantiated parameterized class are shown in Figure 12-6.

Relationship Design in the ESU Course Registration Problem
The following relationships must be designed for the *Add a Course to Teach* scenario:

- ProfessorCourseOptions to AddACourseOffering
- ProfessorCourseOptions to ValidIDList
- AddACourseOffering to Course
- Course to CourseOffering
- CourseOffering to ProfessorInformation
- CourseOffering to DBCourseOffering

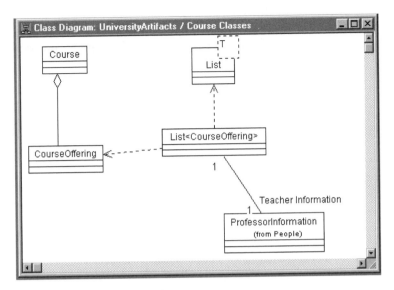

Figure 12-6 Parameterized Classes

ProfessorCourseOptions to AddACourseOffering

As previously mentioned, the actual design of the GUI class AddACourseOffering is dependent upon the set of GUI controls chosen. The designers have chosen to make the relationship an aggregation by value relationship since the lifetimes of the two windows are dependent. The relationship is navigable from the AddACourseOffering class to the Course class.

ProfessorCourseOptions to ValidIDList

The ValidIDList is used by many of the windows to validate the input of a user id. The designers have decided to make this relationship a unidirectional association from ProfessorCourseOptions to ValidIDList.

AddACourseOffering to Course

This is also a GUI class. The designers have chosen to make the relationship navigable from the AddACourseOffering class to the Course class.

Course to CourseOffering

The relationship is unidirectional from Course to CourseOffering since all messages are in that direction. Additionally, the aggregation is by value since all communication with the CourseOffering class is directed through the Course class.

This design implies that a Course and a CourseOffering do not have independent lives. As the requirements for this scenario are stated, this is okay. But, let's look at the idea of a Transcript for a student. If a Transcript is just a pointer to the CourseOfferings that a student has taken, this design does not work—the CourseOffering and the Course would have to have independent lives (and the aggregation would be set to "by reference"). Thus, here is a relationship that may mature as more scenarios are designed.

CourseOffering to ProfessorInformation

The design based on only this scenario would indicate that the relationship should be a dependency relationship between Course-Offering and ProfessorInformation since the ProfessorInformation object is a parameter of the addProfessor operation of the Course-Offering class. However, another scenario for this use case is *Review Schedule*. Here, the ProfessorInformation object must know the related CourseOffering objects, which would imply that the relationship is not a dependency relationship. Finally, the *Create Catalog* scenario needs to know the assigned professor for each Course-Offering. This implies that navigation from CourseOffering to ProfessorInformation is needed. Based on this information, the relationship is not changed—it is a bidirectional association.

CourseOffering to DBCourseOffering

This relationship may be matured into a dependency relationship since the DBCourseOffering is passed a CourseOffering object as a parameter to the save operation.

The updated class diagrams showing the relationship design are shown in Figures 12-7 and 12-8. This design will probably change as more use cases and scenarios are developed for the system.

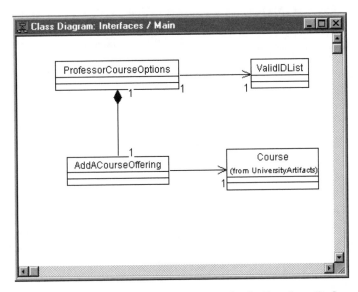

Figure 12-7   Updated Main Class Diagram for the Interfaces Package

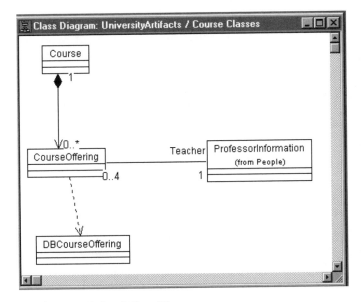

Figure 12-8   Updated Class Diagram

DESIGNING ATTRIBUTES AND OPERATIONS

DURING ANALYSIS, IT was sufficient to specify only attribute and operation names. During design, data types and initial values must be specified for attributes, and operation signatures must be supplied. A data type for an attribute may be a language-supplied type, such as an integer, or it may be a more complex type like a String from a class library. If the attribute must be initialized to a specific value when an object of the class is created, this information is added to the class. In methodology terms, the operation signature includes the parameter list and the return class. Again, parameters and return classes must be assigned a data type. Access control—public, protected, and private—must be set for attributes and operations. Attributes are typically private, but operations may be private or public. If the class is part of an inheritance hierarchy, attributes and operations may be set to protected to allow access to subclasses.

SETTING ATTRIBUTE DATA TYPES
AND INITIAL VALUES IN RATIONAL ROSE

1. Right-click to select the class in the browser or on a class diagram and make the shortcut menu visible.
2. Select the Specification menu choice.
3. Select the Attributes tab.
4. Attributes will have a data type set to type and an initial value set to initval. Click to select the type or initval and place the field in edit mode.
5. Enter the desired data type or initial value.

SETTING OPERATION SIGNATURES IN RATIONAL ROSE

1. Right-click to select the class in the browser or on a class diagram and make the shortcut menu visible.
2. Select the Specification menu choice.
3. Select the Operations tab.
4. Double-click on an operation to make the Operation Specification visible.
5. Enter the return class on the General tab.
6. Select the Detail tab.

7. Right-click on the Arguments field to make the shortcut menu visible.

8. Select the Insert menu choice. This will add an argument. Enter the name, data type, and default value for the argument.

9. Click the OK button to close the Operation Specification.

10. Click the OK button to close the Class Specification.

Note: Attribute and operation detail may also be set on a class diagram by selecting the displayed item and using the following format:

attribute : type = initial value

operation (argname : argtype = default) : return class

Some of the attribute and operation design decisions for the ESU Course Registration problem are shown in Figure 12-9.

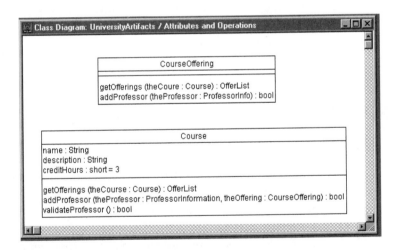

Figure 12-9   Attribute and Operation Design Details

DESIGNING FOR INHERITANCE

DURING ANALYSIS, INHERITANCE hierarchies among key abstractions (i.e., classes) are established. During design, the inheritance hierarchies are refined to:

- Increase reuse
- Incorporate design level classes
- Incorporate chosen library classes

Analysis diagrams are reviewed to identify commonality of attributes, operations, and relationships. Superclasses are defined to hold the newly discovered commonality. This reduces the amount of code to be written and tested. It also enforces uniformity; that is, the same item cannot be handled differently in two different classes if the two classes inherit it from a common superclass.

It is also during this phase of development that polymorphism is added to the model. Polymorphism allows clients to manipulate objects in terms of their common superclasses. That is, an operation will have a defined interface that is used by all of its subclasses, but the subclasses may supply their own implementation of an operation. In order for an operation to be polymorphic in C++, it must be a virtual operation. Often, only the interface is specified in the superclass—there is no code there. This is called a pure virtual function in C++.

CREATING VIRTUAL OPERATIONS IN RATIONAL ROSE

Virtual is a code generation property in Rational Rose.

1. Click the + next to the class in the browser to expand the class.
2. Right-click on the operation to make the shortcut menu visible.
3. Select the Specification menu choice.
4. Select the cg tab.
5. Click to select the value for the property Operation Kind. This will place the value in edit mode.
6. Select virtual to make the operation virtual. Select abstract to make the operation pure virtual.
7. Click the OK button to close the Specification.

The operation specification is shown in Figure 12-10.

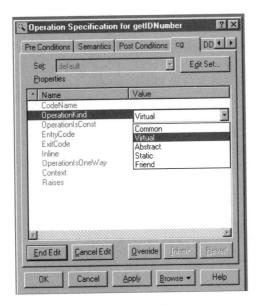

Figure 12-10   Operation Specification

Code Generation and Design

The final step in design of an iteration is to add the methods that every good C++ class needs—for example, constructors, destructors, and copy constructors. These methods can be added by hand, but this entails a lot of typing. This is why the ability to add these types of methods to a class is found in the Rose code generator.

Rational Rose has a very powerful C++ code generation capability. Code is generated based on information obtained from the diagrams, the specifications, and the options specified in the code generation properties for each type of element. A step-by-step guide to code generation with Rational Rose (C++ variant) may be found in Appendix A.

CODING, TESTING, AND DOCUMENTING THE ITERATION

ONE OF THE final steps in building an iteration is the implementation of the method bodies in the chosen language before an iteration is complete. Interaction diagrams (Sequence and Collaboration diagrams) are used to help in this process since they tell you who does what to whom and when they do it.

Testing, although it is has not been discussed until this point, is a very important ingredient in the iterative and incremental life cycle. As analysis and design progresses through the life cycle, testing plans and procedures are created. Again, use cases are an important part of this activity since they document what the system must do. The iteration should be tested to ensure that it truly does what is stated in the use case. Iterations are also integrated with previous iterations—you do not wait until the system is complete to put the iterations together. The iteration is evaluated to ensure that it eliminates its assigned risks. Any risks that are not eliminated (along with any risks that were found along the way) are reassigned to a future iteration.

The decisions made regarding the design of the iteration are captured in the models for the iteration. This information is used to generate the documentation for the iteration. Documentation should be generated on a iterative basis—I have found that systems that wait until the project is complete to document it rarely have good documentation (indeed, they sometimes do not have any documentation!).

USING REVERSE ENGINEERING TO SET THE STAGE FOR THE NEXT ITERATION

THE MODEL MUST be updated to reflect any changes made to the code (e.g., helping methods added, new classes added) while implementing the current iteration. Rather than updating the model by hand, the reverse engineering capability of Rose can be used to generate a model based on the current implementation, and this information can be merged into the model. A step-by-step guide to reverse engineering with Rational Rose (C++ variant) may be found in Appendix B.

SUMMARY

THE ITERATION RELEASE plan prescribes schedules for all the increments of the system. The scenarios developed during analysis are the main input to this phase of development. The scenarios are examined and prioritized according to risk, importance to the customer, and the need to develop certain basic scenarios first. As each iteration is completed, risks are re-evaluated and the project plan is updated as needed.

Earlier in the project life cycle, placeholder classes were created for the boundary classes for the system. Now these classes must be finalized—number of windows, window layout, and handling events from users. Classes typically are added to the model to facilitate the how of a system. Patterns provide the capability to reuse successful designs and architectures, which leads to more maintainable systems and increased productivity. As with any classes developed at this point in the life cycle, the classes created to instantiate the design pattern are added to the model and the class diagram. Relationship design decisions include navigation, containment, refinement, and multiplicity implementation. Attribute data types and initial values are specified, and operation signatures are finalized. Analysis level diagrams are examined to determine if any inheritance may be added to the model. Operations in inheritance hierarchies are analyzed to determine if any polymorphism exists. If so, the operation is made either virtual or pure virtual.

The final step of design for an iteration is to add the methods that every good C++ class needs—for example, constructors, destructors, and copy constructors. Rational Rose has a very powerful C++ code generation capability. Code is generated based on information obtained from the diagrams, the specifications, and the options specified in the code generation properties for each type of element.

Finally, the method bodies are implemented in the chosen language. Each iteration should be tested and documented before it is considered completed. The iteration is evaluated, and any unmitigated risks are assigned to a future release.

Appendix A

Round-Trip Engineering
with Rational Rose/C++

THIS APPENDIX CONTAINS a step-by-step guide to code generation and reverse engineering with Rational Rose/C + +.

Code Generation Steps

Step 1: Create Needed Property Sets
Step 2: Create Body Components in the Component Diagram
Step 3: Attach Property Sets to Classes
Step 4: Select the Components and Generate the Code
Step 5: Evaluate the Code Generation Errors

Reverse Engineering Steps

Step 1: Create a Project
Step 2: Add Project Caption
Step 3: Add Referenced Libraries and Base Projects
Step 4: Set the File Type and Analyze the Files
Step 5: Evaluate the Errors
Step 6: Select Export Options and Export to Rose
Step 7: Update Rose Model

CODE GENERATION

Step 1: Create Needed Property Sets

There are code generation properties associated with the project, the class, the roles, attributes, and operations. The properties applying to the project as a whole involve file name, default container names, and placement of the generated code. Class properties involve the generation of constructors, destructors, copy constructors, equality operators, and get/set methods. The property set for roles deals with the construction of get/set methods, visibility of the methods, and the container class to be used. Operation properties deal with the operation kind (common, virtual, abstract, static, or friend), and allow the operation to be made constant. These property sets may be edited, and new sets may be created to specify the C + + features needed for the project. Two files are generated for each class—a header (.h) file and a specification (.cpp) file.

For a typical project, a few people are responsible for the creation of code generation property sets that are used by the entire development team. This enables each developer to generate the needed code for the components. Some typical property sets are: Virtual destructor, Virtual operation, Abstract operation, Static operation, No get member function, and Forward reference.

CREATING PROPERTY SETS IN RATIONAL ROSE

1. Select the Tools:Options menu choice.
2. Select the cg tab.
3. Click the arrow on the Type field to make the drop-down menu visible.
4. Select the desired type of property set.
5. Click the Clone button to make the Clone Property Set window visible.
6. Enter the name of the new property set.
7. Click the OK button to close the Clone Property Set window.
8. Click to select the property to change.
9. Click the Edit Value button to place the property in edit mode.
10. Enter the new value or select the new value from the drop-down menu if one is provided.
11. Repeat steps 8 through 10 for each property to be changed.
12. Click the Apply button to apply the changes.
13. Repeat the preceding steps for each new property set.
14. Click the OK button to close the Options window.

The property set Virtual Destructor is shown in Figure A-1.

Step 2: Create Body Components in the Component Diagram

If a class is mapped to a component, Rational Rose generates code based on the type of components present in the diagram. If there is only a component representing the header file, Rose will generate only an .h file containing definition information for the class. If there

Figure A-1   Virtual Destructor Property Set

is a corresponding component representing the body, Rose will generate a .cpp file containing declaration information for the class. If a class is mapped to a component representing the body, Rose will generate one file containing definition and declaration information for the class. The component that is used to represent the body is not added to the component diagram toolbar by default—you must customize the toolbar.

CUSTOMIZING THE DIAGRAM TOOLBAR IN RATIONAL ROSE

1. Right-click on the toolbar to make the shortcut menu visible.
2. Select the Customize menu choice.
3. Select the icon representing a package body.
4. Select the Add - > button.
5. Click the Close button to close the Customize Toolbar window.

The Customize Toolbar window is shown in Figure A-2.

Figure A-2   *Customize Toolbar Window*

Component bodies are added to the model for the components created during architecture design—if a component body is not present, Rose/C++ will generate only an .h file (it will not generate a .cpp file). Dependency relationships are added between the body and the specification.

CREATING COMPONENT BODIES IN RATIONAL ROSE

1. Double-click on a component diagram to open the diagram.
2. Click to select the Package Body icon on the toolbar.
3. Click to place the Package Body icon on the diagram.
4. While the body is still selected, enter the name of the body—this is typically the same name as the name of the specification.
5. Click to select the Dependency icon on the toolbar.
6. Click on the package body in the diagram, and drag the dependency to the package specification.

An updated component diagram is shown in Figure A-3.

Step 3: Attach Property Sets to Classes

Each class is examined to determine its code needs. If a property set exists, it is attached to the class.

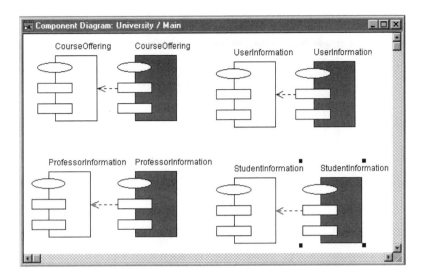

Figure A-3   Updated Component Diagram

ATTACHING A PROPERTY SET TO A
SELECTED ELEMENT IN RATIONAL ROSE

1. Right-click to select the element in the Browser or on a diagram and make the shortcut menu visible.
2. Select the Specification menu choice.
3. Select the cg tab.
4. Click the arrow on the Set field to make the drop-down menu visible.
5. Select the desired property set.
6. Click the OK button to close the Specification.

The property set VirtualDestructor has been attached to the UserInformation class as shown in Figure A-4.

Since there are not property sets for every combination of elements, any property may also be overridden for a particular element. This is true even if the property is part of the default property set for the element.

Figure A-4   Property Set Attachment

OVERRIDING A PROPERTY IN RATIONAL ROSE

1. Right-click to select the element in the Browser or on a diagram and make the shortcut menu visible.
2. Select the Specification menu choice.
3. Select the cg tab.
4. Click the arrow on the Set field to make the drop-down menu visible.
5. Select the desired property set.
6. Click to select the value to be changed.
7. Click the Edit Value button to place the property in edit mode.
8. Enter the new value or select the new value from the drop-down menu if one is provided.
9. Repeat steps 6 through 8 for each property to be changed.
10. Click the OK button to close the Specification.

Step 4: Select the Components and Generate the Code

Code may be generated for an entire package, a class, or a set of classes. If a class is not mapped to a component, the name of the class is used to generate the name of the file containing the code. The code is placed in a directory structure that corresponds to the package names in the logical view. If a class is mapped to a component, the name of the component is used to generate the name of the file containing the code. The code is placed in a directory structure that corresponds to the package names in the component view.

GENERATING CODE IN RATIONAL ROSE

1. Click to select the package, class, or set of classes.
2. Select the Tools:C++:Code Generation menu choice.
3. Rose will display the status in the Code Generation Status window.

The Code Generation Status window is shown in Figure A-5.

Figure A-5   Code Generation Status Window

Step 5: Evaluate the Code Generation Errors

Rose writes all warnings and errors to the Log window. If part of the design for the class is not complete, Rose will write a warning message to the log and use a default value. This is especially important if an iterative approach to development is being followed since an entire class may not be implemented in one iteration.

The common warnings and errors output from the code generator are:

- Error: missing attribute data type; void is assumed
- Warning: unspecified multiplicity/cardinality indicators; one is assumed
- Warning: missing operation return type; void is assumed

A sample of the code generated for the Course class is found in Appendix B.

REVERSE ENGINEERING USING THE C + + ANALYZER

Step 1: Create a Project

A C + + Analyzer project contains the information needed to extract a Rose design from source-code files. An analyzer project contains the following information:

- Caption: informational description of the project
- Directories: list of directories used by the Analyzer (the directories that contain the source code files, as well as the directories containing any code used by the source code to be analyzed, must be included in the directory list)
- Extensions: list of file extensions recognized by the analyzer
- Files: list of files to be analyzed
- Defined Symbols and Undefined Symbols: list of preprocessor symbols and their expansions

- Categories: list of packages to which classes and packages may be assigned
- Subsystems: list of packages to which components and packages may be assigned
- Bases: list of base projects containing information needed to resolve source code references
- Type 2 Context: preprocessor directives needed by context-sensitive source code files
- Export Options: list of information that is to be exported either to create or update a Rose model

Once a project is created, it is saved with a .pjt extension.

CREATING A PROJECT IN THE C++ ANALYZER

1. Select the Tools:C++:Reverse Engineering menu choice to start the C++ Analyzer.
2. Select the File:New menu choice.

The C++ Analyzer Project window is shown in Figure A-6.

Step 2: Add Project Caption

Just as code is documented for future use, analyzer projects are also documented. Each project should contain a caption. Typically, this is descriptive information about the project (such as its title and purpose) that may be used by other teams to determine if the project has reuse potential either as a standalone project or as a base project.

ADDING A CAPTION IN THE C++ ANALYZER

1. Click the Caption button to make the Caption window visible.
2. Enter the information in the Caption window.
3. Click the OK button to close the Caption window.

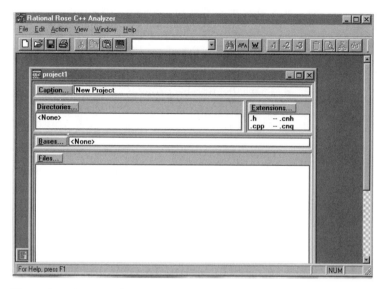

Figure A-6   C++ Analyzer Project Window

The Caption window is shown in Figure A-7.

Figure A-7   Caption Window

Step 3: Add Referenced Libraries and Base Projects

The directory list contains a list of directories used by the C++
Analyzer. The directory containing a file to be analyzed must be in
the directory list. In addition, the directory for any included file must
also be in the directory list.

CREATING THE DIRECTORY LIST IN THE C++ ANALYZER

1. Click the Directories button to make the Project Directory List window visible.
2. Click to select a directory in the Directory Structure file. This will set the directory to the current directory.
3. Click the Add Current button to add the current directory to the directory list.
4. Click the Add Subdirs button to add the current directory and its immediate subdirectories to the directory list.
5. Click the Add Hierarchy button to add the current directory and all its nested subdirectories to the directory list.

The Project Directory List window is shown in Figure A-8.

Figure A-8   Project Directory List Window

An analyzer project may use information from another project, called a base project. Typically, base projects contain information about header files for compiler-specific libraries or class libraries on which the program is built. Rather than reanalyze this information in every project that uses these files, a base project is created. The base project may then be used by any other project that needs information about the files in the base project. Base projects are identified in the base project list.

If the Analyzer cannot find a file in the project directory list, it will look for the file in a base project. Base projects are searched in the order in which they appear in the base project list.

ADDING BASE PROJECTS IN THE C++ ANALYZER

1. Click the Bases button to make the Base Projects window visible.
2. Click to navigate through the directory structure until the desired project is visible in the File Name box.
3. Click to select the project.
4. Click the Add button to add the base project.

The Base Projects window is shown in Figure A-9.

Figure A-9   Base Projects Window

Step 4: Set the File Type and Analyze the Files

The Analyzer categorizes files into three different file types—Type 1, Type 2, and Type 3. When a file is added to the file list, it is made a Type 1 file. This type of file is syntactically complete and context independent; that is, the file is a list of complete C++ declarations at file scope and either contains all information that it needs or obtains the information from its #include directives. A Type 2 file is syntactically complete but context dependent; that is, the file is a list of complete C++ declarations at file scope, but the file contains symbols whose definitions are provided by the context in which it is included. A Type 3 file is syntactically incomplete. Type 3 files are always processed as they are encountered.

TO CHANGE THE ANALYSIS TYPE IN THE C++ ANALYZER

1. Click to select the file in the files list.
2. Click to select the appropriate type from the Action:Set Type menu.

The C++ Analyzer may process a single file or a group of files. The Analyzer creates and stores analysis information in a data file for each file it processes. This data may be used the next time the file is analyzed. The status of each file is updated in the files list as the file is processed. The status may be:

- Unknown: the file has not been analyzed.

- Stale data: there is potentially out-of-date data for the file.

- Analyzed: successful analysis; this status is applied to Type 1 and Type 2 source code files only.

- CodeCycled: successful analysis, and the file contains annotations that protect existing information in the code from being overwritten. This status is applied to Type 1 and Type 2 source code files only.

- Excluded: this is a Type 3 file, which is analyzed each time it is encountered in another file.

- Has errors: found errors in the source code file while analyzing it.

- No source: cannot find the file in the file system.

- Unanalyzed: cannot find a data file for this file.

ANALYZING FILES IN THE C++ ANALYZER

1. Set the Analysis Type for each file to be analyzed.
2. Click to select the files in the files list.
3. Select the Action:Analyze menu choice to analyze the file, or select the Action:Code Cycle menu choice to analyze the file and ensure that the annotations needed for Rose are present.

The Analyzer window, along with an analysis status, is shown in Figure A-10.

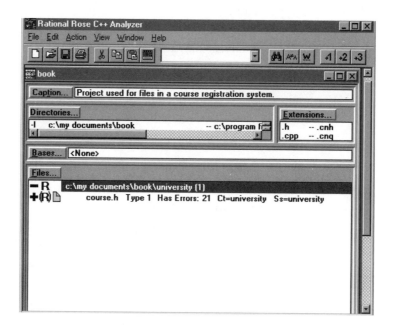

Figure A-10   Analyzer Status

Step 5: Evaluate the Errors

The Analyzer writes all errors to the Log window. Errors can also be viewed in the files list by double-clicking on the file. Each error should be evaluated as to its severity. Some common errors are:

- Unresolved references: the Analyzer cannot find referenced source files. To resolve this type of error, the directory containing the referenced source file must be added to the directory list.

- Missing language extensions: language extensions not recognized by the Analyzer. To resolve this type of error, the language extension must be defined as a symbol.

- Context-sensitive source files: code from another directory is referenced but not included in the file. To resolve this type of error, change the file to either a Type 2 or a Type 3 file.

The analyzer window, along with the errors encountered during analysis, is shown in Figure A-11.

Step 6: Select Export Options and Export to Rose

The export options specify what elements should be modeled and drawn in the exported file. For example, a class can be modeled and drawn, comments can be added, associations can be modeled and drawn, and dependency relationships can be modeled. If an element is modeled and drawn, it will be visible in the created or updated Rose model. If an element is modeled, it can be drawn within Rose once a Rose model is created or updated. If it is not modeled, then it can never be drawn in Rose.

The C++ Analyzer has multiple export-option sets already set up for your use. They are:

- Round-trip: export options useful in a round-trip engineering exercise. A file with the extension .red is created.

- First look: high-level look at the model. An .mdl file is created.

Figure A-11   Analyzer Errors

- DetailedAnalysis: detailed look at the model. An .mdl file
  is created.

You have the option of using one of the pre-existing export-option sets, modifying one of the pre-existing export-option sets, or creating your own export-option set.

EXPORTING TO ROSE IN THE C++ ANALYZER

1. Click to select the files to be exported.
2. Select the Action:Export to Rose menu choice.
3. Click the arrow on the Option Set field to make the drop-down menu visible.
4. Click to select the desired export-option set.
5. Click the OK button or the Overwrite button to export to Rose.

The Export to Rose window is shown in Figure A-12.

Figure A-12   Export to Rose Window

Step 7: Update Rose Model

Once the .red file is created by the Analyzer, it is used to update the Rose model. This will replace elements of the Rose model with elements extracted from the source code. In addition, any elements in the code that are not in the model are added to the model.

UPDATING A ROSE MODEL

1. Open the Rose model to be updated.
2. Select the File:Update menu choice.
3. Navigate through the directory structure to locate the .red file.
4. Click to select the .red file.
5. Click the OK button to close the Update Model From window.

Appendix B

Sample Code Generated by Rational Rose/C++

Course.h

```
//## begin module.cm preserve=no
//        %X% %Q% %Z% %W%
//## end module.cm

//## begin module.cp preserve=no
//## end module.cp

//## Module: Course; Pseudo Package specification
//## Subsystem: University
//## Source file:
        c:\my documents\book\University\Course.h

#ifndef Course_h
#define Course_h 1

//## begin module.additionalIncludes preserve=no
//## end module.additionalIncludes

//## begin module.includes preserve=yes
//## end module.includes

// ProfessorCourseManager
#include "University\ProfessorCourseManager.h"

//## begin module.additionalDeclarations preserve=yes
//## end module.additionalDeclarations

//## Class: Course
// A class offered by the University.
//## Category: UniversityArtifacts
//## Subsystem: University
//## Persistence: Transient
//## Cardinality/Multiplicity: n

class Course
{
  //## begin Course.initialDeclarations preserve=yes
  //## end Course.initialDeclarations

  public:
    //## Constructors (generated)
      Course();

      Course(const Course &right);

    //## Destructor (generated)
      ~Course();
```

```
//## Assignment Operation (generated)
 const Course & operator=(const Course &right);

//## Equality Operations (generated)
 int operator==(const Course &right) const;

 int operator!=(const Course &right) const;


//## Other Operations (specified)
 //## Operation: getOfferings%866004058
 OfferList getOfferings(Course theCourse);

 //## Operation: addProfessor%866004059
 // Add a professor as the teacher of a particular course
 // offering of the course.
 //
 // Inputs:  professor and course offering
 // Outputs:  success indicator
 bool addProfessor(ProfessorInformation theProfessor,
CourseOffering theOffering);

 //## Operation: validateProfessor%866004060
 bool validateProfessor();

//## Get and Set Operations for Associations (generated)

 //## Association: manages%33764D8801CC
 //## Role: Course::<the_ProfessorCourseManager>
 const ProfessorCourseManager
get_the_ProfessorCourseManager() const;
 void set_the_ProfessorCourseManager(const
ProfessorCourseManager value);

// Additional Public Declarations
 //## begin Course.public preserve=yes
 //## end Course.public


protected:
 // Additional Protected Declarations
 //## begin Course.protected preserve=yes
 //## end Course.protected

private:
 //## Get and Set Operations for Class Attributes (generated)
```

```
//## Attribute: name
// The title of the course that is used in all University
// publications.
const String get_name() const;
void set_name(const String value);

//## Attribute: description
const String get_description() const;
void set_description(const String value);

//## Attribute: creditHours
const short get_creditHours() const;
void set_creditHours(const short value);

// Additional Private Declarations
//## begin Course.private preserve=yes
//## end Course.private

private: //## implementation
// Data Members for Class Attributes

//## begin Course::name.attr preserve=no  private: String {U}
String name;
//## end Course::name.attr

//## begin Course::description.attr preserve=no  private:
String {U}
String description;
//## end Course::description.attr

//## begin Course::creditHours.attr preserve=no  private:
short {U} 3
short creditHours;
//## end Course::creditHours.attr

// Data Members for Associations

//## Association: manages%33764D8801CC
//## begin Course::<the_ProfessorCourseManager>.role
preserve=no  public: ProfessorCourseManager { -> UHN}
ProfessorCourseManager the_ProfessorCourseManager;
//## end Course::<the_ProfessorCourseManager>.role

//## Association: <unnamed>%337651230398
//## Role: Course::<the_CourseOffering>
//## begin Course::<the_CourseOffering>.role preserve=no
public: CourseOffering { -> UH}
//## end Course::<the_CourseOffering>.role
```

```
      //## Association: <unnamed>%33AF4FCE0104
      //## Role: Course::<the_AddACourseOffering>
      //## begin Course::<the_AddACourseOffering>.role
  preserve=no  public: AddACourseOffering {1 -> UH}
      //## end Course::<the_AddACourseOffering>.role

    // Additional Implementation Declarations
      //## begin Course.implementation preserve=yes
      //## end Course.implementation
  };

  // Class Course

  //## Get and Set Operations for Class Attributes (inline)

  inline const String Course::get_name() const
  {
    //## begin Course::get_name%.get preserve=no
    return name;
    //## end Course::get_name%.get
  }

  inline void Course::set_name(const String value)
  {
    //## begin Course::set_name%.set preserve=no
    name = value;
    //## end Course::set_name%.set
  }

  inline const String Course::get_description() const
  {
    //## begin Course::get_description%.get preserve=no
    return description;
    //## end Course::get_description%.get
  }

  inline void Course::set_description(const String value)
  {
    //## begin Course::set_description%.set preserve=no
    description = value;
    //## end Course::set_description%.set
  }

  inline const short Course::get_creditHours() const
  {
    //## begin Course::get_creditHours%.get preserve=no
    return creditHours;
    //## end Course::get_creditHours%.get
  }
```

```
inline void Course::set_creditHours(const short value)
{
  //## begin Course::set_creditHours%.set preserve=no
  creditHours = value;
  //## end Course::set_creditHours%.set
}

//## Get and Set Operations for Associations (inline)

inline const ProfessorCourseManager
    Course::get_the_ProfessorCourseManager() const
{
  //## begin Course::get_the_ProfessorCourseManager%.get
    preserve=no
  return the_ProfessorCourseManager;
  //## end Course::get_the_ProfessorCourseManager%.get
}

inline void Course::set_the_ProfessorCourseManager(const
    ProfessorCourseManager value)
{
  //## begin Course::set_the_ProfessorCourseManager%.set
    preserve=no
  the_ProfessorCourseManager = value;
  //## end Course::set_the_ProfessorCourseManager%.set
}

#endif
```

Course.cpp

```
//## begin module.cm preserve=no
//          %X% %Q% %Z% %W%
//## end module.cm

//## begin module.cp preserve=no
//## end module.cp

//## Module: Course; Pseudo Package body
//## Subsystem: University
//## Source file:
c:\my          documents\book\University\Course.cpp

//## begin module.additionalIncludes preserve=no
//## end module.additionalIncludes
```

```
//## begin module.includes preserve=yes
//## end module.includes

// Course
#include "University\Course.h"

//## begin module.additionalDeclarations preserve=yes
//## end module.additionalDeclarations

// Class Course

Course::Course()
  //## begin Course::Course%.hasinit preserve=no
    : creditHours(3)
  //## end Course::Course%.hasinit
  //## begin Course::Course%.initialization preserve=yes
  //## end Course::Course%.initialization
{
  //## begin Course::Course%.body preserve=yes
  //## end Course::Course%.body
}


Course::Course(const Course &right)
  //## begin Course::Course%copy.hasinit preserve=no
    : creditHours(3)
  //## end Course::Course%copy.hasinit
  //## begin Course::Course%copy.initialization preserve=yes
  //## end Course::Course%copy.initialization
{
  //## begin Course::Course%copy.body preserve=yes
  //## end Course::Course%copy.body
}


Course::~Course()
{
  //## begin Course::~Course%.body preserve=yes
  //## end Course::~Course%.body
}

const Course & Course::operator=(const Course &right)
{
  //## begin Course::operator=%.body preserve=yes
  //## end Course::operator=%.body
}


int Course::operator==(const Course &right) const
{
  //## begin Course::operator==%.body preserve=yes
  //## end Course::operator==%.body
}
```

```
int Course::operator!=(const Course &right) const
{
  //## begin Course::operator!=%.body preserve=yes
  //## end Course::operator!=%.body
}

//## Other Operations (implementation)
OfferList Course::getOfferings(Course theCourse)
{
  //## begin Course::getOfferings%866004058.body preserve=yes
  //## end Course::getOfferings%866004058.body
}

bool Course::addProfessor(ProfessorInformation theProfessor,
    CourseOffering theOffering)
{
  //## begin Course::addProfessor%866004059.body
preserve=yes
  //## end Course::addProfessor%866004059.body
}

bool Course::validateProfessor()
{
  //## begin Course::validateProfessor%866004060.body
preserve=yes
  //## end Course::validateProfessor%866004060.body
}

// Additional Declarations
//## begin Course.declarations preserve=yes
//## end Course.declarations
```

Glossary

ACTION
> Behavior that accompanies a transition event. An action is considered to take zero time and cannot be interrupted.

ACTIVITY
> Behavior that occurs while in a state. An activity can be interrupted by a transition event.

ACTOR
> Someone or something external to the system that must interact with the system under development.

AGGREGATION
> A stronger form of an association where the relationship is between a whole and its part(s).

ARCHITECTURE
> The logical and physical structure of a system, forged by all the strategic and tactical design decisions applied during development.

ASSOCIATION
> A bidirectional, semantic connection between two classes.

ASSOCIATION CLASS
> A class that holds information belonging to a link between two objects, not with one object by itself.

ATTRIBUTE
> A data definition held by objects of a class. The structure of the class.

AUTOMATIC TRANSITION
> A transition that occurs automatically after the activity within the originating state is completed.

BACKGROUND PROBLEM STATEMENT

Cumulative background material assembled before working on a project. It often includes a description and critique of the previous system.

BASE PROJECT

A project that supplements the information in a program-specific project, usually with information about header files for compiler-specific libraries or other class libraries being used.

BUSINESS GOALS

Prioritized statements of the organization's needs, used to guide decision making and trade-off throughout the development process.

CLASS

A description of a group of objects with common properties (attributes), common behavior (operations), common relationships to other objects (associations and aggregations), and common semantics.

CLASS DIAGRAM

A view or picture of some or all of the classes in a model.

CLASS LIBRARY

A library consisting of classes that may be used by other developers.

COLLABORATION DIAGRAM

A diagram that shows object interactions organized around the objects and their links to each other.

COMPONENT DIAGRAM

A diagram that shows the organizations and dependencies among software components, including source code components, run-time components, and executable components.

CONSISTENCY CHECKING

The process of ensuring that information in both the static view of the system (class diagrams) and the dynamic view of the system (sequence and collaboration diagrams) are telling the same story.

CONSTRUCTION

Building the product as a series of incremental iterations.

CONTROLLED UNIT

A package that can be loaded or saved independently and integrated into a configuration management system.

DEPLOYMENT DIAGRAM

A diagram used to show the allocation of processes to nodes in the physical design of a system.

DESIGN

How the system will be realized in the implementation phase.

ELABORATION

Planning the necessary activities and required resources; specifying the features and designing the architecture.

GENERALIZATION

The process used to create superclasses that encapsulate structure and behavior common to several classes.

GUARD

A condition that must evaluate to TRUE in order for a specified transition to occur.

IMPLEMENTATION

The production of the code that will result in an executable system.

INCEPTION

The specification of the project vision.

INHERITANCE

A relationship among classes where one class shares the structure and/or behavior defined in one or more other classes.

ITERATION PLAN

The schedule of the iterative releases planned for a system.

ITERATIVE AND INCREMENTAL LIFE CYCLE

The development of a series of architectural releases that evolves into the final system.

KEY MECHANISM

A design decision that has local architectural implications.

LAYER

The collection of packages at the same level of abstraction.

MODEL

An abstraction that portrays the essentials of a complex problem or structure, making it easier to manipulate.

OBJECT

A concept, abstraction, or thing with sharp boundaries and meaning for an application.

OPERATION

Work that one object performs upon another to elicit a reaction. The behavior of the class.

PARTITION

The packages that form part of a given level of abstraction.

POLYMORPHISM
> Provides the capability for clients to manipulate objects in terms of their common superclasses.

PROOF OF CONCEPT PROTOTYPE
> The prototype used to validate the initial assumptions stated for a given problem space.

REQUIREMENTS ANALYSIS
> The description of what the system should do.

SCENARIO
> An instance of a use case—it is one path through the flow of events for the use case.

SEQUENCE DIAGRAM
> A diagram that depicts object interactions arranged in time sequence.

SPECIALIZATION
> The process used to create subclasses that represent refinements in which structure and/or behavior are added, modified, or even hidden.

STATE
> The cumulative results of the behavior of an object; one of the possible conditions in which an object may exist.

STATE TRANSITION
> The passing from one state to another.

STATE TRANSITION DIAGRAM
> A diagram used to show the state space of a given class, the events that cause a transition from one state to another, and the actions that result from a state change.

STEREOTYPE

A new type of modeling element that extends the meta-model. Stereotypes must be based on elements that are part of the UML metamodel.

SUBCLASS

A class that inherits from one or more classes.

SUPERCLASS

The class from which another class inherits.

TEST

The verification of the entire system.

TRANSITION

Supplying the product to the user community (manufacturing, delivering, and training).

UNIFIED MODELING LANGUAGE (UML)

A language used to specify, visualize, and document the artifacts of an object-oriented system under development.

USE CASE

Representation of the business processes of the system. The model of a dialogue between an actor and the system.

USE CASE DIAGRAM

A graphical representation of some or all of the actors, use cases, and their interactions.

USE CASE MODEL

The collection of actors, use cases, and use case diagrams for a system.

VISUAL MODELING

A way of thinking about problems using models organized around real-world ideas.

Index